"In its clear, inviting, and practical way, this book can change your life. Drawing on her years of combining mindfulness with the expansive power of compassion, Radhule Weininger brings us practices that serve to free us from fear, despair, self-hate, and other oppressive mind states. Her three-part book begins with the rare, poignant journey that led her to these discoveries, and then, after their various forms are carefully set forth, concludes with nine real-life stories of how different people have put them to use. *Heartwork* helps me to be more present in each moment, more mindful of each encounter."

—JOANNA MACY, author of *Coming Back to Life*

"Conveyed through prose that is accessible to readers from a range of spiritual traditions and backgrounds, Weininger presents her insights on the methods she has found useful for identifying the roots of the issues we are all grappling with, as a first step toward addressing them through practice and perseverance. Shining through every chapter is the author's desire to help reduce the suffering that is the common thread connecting humanity."

—VICTOR CHAN, coauthor of *The Wisdom of Compassion*
with His Holiness the Fourteenth Dalai Lama

"*Heartwork* is a beautifully written, reader-friendly guide to practical mindfulness. It makes compassion a livable rule of life in a challenging world."

—THOMAS MOORE, author of *Care of the Soul*

"Weininger, a gifted therapist and a practiced Buddhist, shares *how* we can nourish compassion in our daily lives. Take time with this wise book and engage its guided meditations and queries to help ground your life in the wellsprings of compassion."

—MARY WATKINS, PhD,
author of *Toward Psychologies of Liberation*

D0011769

Heartwork

The Path of Self-Compassion

RADHULE WEININGER, MD, PhD

Foreword by Jack Kornfield

SHAMBHALA Boulder 2017

Shambhala Publications, Inc.
4720 Walnut Street
Boulder, Colorado 80301
www.shambhala.com

9 8 7 6 5 4 3 2 1

First Edition

Printed in the United States of America

♾ This edition is printed on acid-free paper that meets the American National
Standards Institute Z39.48 Standard.
♻ This book was printed on 30% post-consumer recycled paper. For more infor-
mation please visit www.shambhala.com.

Distributed in the United States by Penguin Random House LLC and in Canada
by Random House of Canada Ltd

Designed by Greta D. Sibley

Library of Congress Cataloging-in-Publication Data
Names: Weininger, Radhule, author.
Title: Heartwork: the path of self-compassion / Radhule Weininger, MD, PhD;
    foreword by Jack Kornfield.
Description: First Edition. | Boulder: Shambhala Publications, 2017. |
    Includes bibliographical references and index.
Identifiers: LCCN 2016041457 | ISBN 9781611804812 (pbk.; alk. paper)
Subjects: LCSH: Compassion. | Love. | Forgiveness.
Classification: LCC BJ1475 .W45 2017 | DDC 158.1—dc23
LC record available at https://lccn.loc.gov/2016041457

DEDICATION

I am dedicating this book to H.H. the Dalai Lama and his tireless efforts to make our world a better place. Earlier this month I had the wonderful opportunity to talk to him in person. He was surprisingly firm with me as he said, "You are a psychologist. I want you to teach how to deal with difficult emotions, not as a religion but as a science of the Mind."

When I told him that I have been working to make his teachings accessible, relevant, and easy for those I work with, the Dalai Lama answered, "That's very good, very important work. Do more of that."

This felt like a strong endorsement of what I want to do in this book: use the power of compassion to help us face what is hard to look at, the difficult spaces within ourselves. As we become increasingly well and able to live with ease, it is my strong conviction that our world will become a happier, healthier place.

The work of the eyes is done. Now, go and do the heart work.

—*Rainer Maria Rilke*

CONTENTS

PART THREE *Stories*

FOREWORD

Heartwork is a beautiful and encouraging book. It offers a compass, a map, a guide to help us navigate the tender, and at times difficult, passages of life. It spells out how we can hold ourselves and others with compassion and understanding. Its greatest gift is its practicality; it offers direct help to the heart.

Without the kind of inner understanding found in this book, we can go through life tossed about like a boat without a rudder. Zorba says, "Trouble? Life is trouble." In our human incarnation, we get to experience it all. A magenta sunrise over the Grand Canyon, a lime-green caterpillar climbing the champagne-pink blossoms of a peony, the shy smile illuminating the eyes of a child. We each will know connection and longing, intimacy and loneliness. We will have personal struggles and conflicts, and the troubled world is with us—the streams of weary refugees; the endangered animals; the continuing wars and injustice; and the despair, fear, and anger. All the while, modern media and commercialism will try to frighten us or entice and soothe us.

How can we navigate through it all? The answer is found in the potential of the human heart. Your heart can grow in empathy, compassion, and love, no matter what the circumstances of your life! This truth is not just the simple recitation of a perennial ideal, such as "love your neighbor as yourself." It is a powerful call to your innermost dignity and wisdom, and most important, it is a method of practice to learn how to do it. Remember that just as Nelson Mandela walked out of the South African prison on Robben Island after twenty-seven years with forgiveness, dignity, and compassion, you can walk out of your prisons too. Whether it is past hurt and trauma, unworthiness and shame, or anger and outer conflict, it can be healed and improved with compassion. Your heart is fundamentally free. No one can imprison your spirit.

Years ago, a number of us—Western psychologists and teachers— met with the Dalai Lama. When we asked him for help dealing with the self-hatred and inner criticism so common in Western students, the Dalai Lama was confused. There is no word for self-hatred in Tibetan, and he spent a long time just trying to understand what we meant. He asked if the teachers present experienced this self-hatred, and many raised their hands. After some quiet reflection, he looked around at us with eyes of great compassion and said, "But this is a mistake." Compassion must include yourself as well as others.

Heartwork is full of the perfect practices to teach you how to develop this compassion. With compelling stories and a spirit of wisdom, forgiveness, and honesty, Radhule Weininger offers you gifts to change your life.

> Read *Heartwork* slowly.
> Savor its wisdom.
> Journal with it. Practice with it.
> Adapt the practices and phrases to make it your own.
> Let it become a heartfelt conversation with your soul.
>
> May the compassion you awaken bring great blessings
> to you
> and all you touch.

—*Jack Kornfield*
Spirit Rock Center,
Woodacre, California 2017

INTRODUCTION

May I hold myself gently and with care. May I regard myself with understanding and compassion.

Christina settled her left hand on her chest, close to her heart. After a long exhalation, she rested her right hand on top of her left. I knew that Christina had been wounded in significant ways, yet she had buried many unexpressed feelings deep inside. Worry that she would be overwhelmed by her fears and a pervasive sense of shame had prevented Christina from seeking the help she needed until now.

May I be free from shame. May I extend compassion toward this bruised heart of mine. May I forgive you as I forgive myself. May all those in this world who suffer from humiliation and dismay be free.

Sitting in the big brown leather chair in my office, Christina told me about her early life during the civil war in Argentina. Hidden in the trunk of a car, five-year-old Christina miraculously survived while militia murdered her mother. Growing up, Christina was treated harshly by her stepmother, who only reluctantly accepted the girl into her father's house. She lived a Cinderella-like existence until she was twenty-one and she had the chance to move to America. As Christina told me her wrenching history, I sensed that a practice in self-compassion would help her contain and work with her profound suffering.

My work with Christina began when her cardiologist sent her to me. He thought she would benefit from seeing a psychotherapist and mindfulness meditation teacher who worked with compassion practices. Christina had recently experienced a scary attack of cardiac arrhythmia. While she was driving on the highway, her heart began beating rapidly, as if an electrical current were racing through her chest. She pulled the car to the side of the road just in time. Her heart stopped and skipped a beat before starting up again.

Christina's cardiologist explained to her that her heart had a special vulnerability, and her symptoms had likely been set off by stress or strong emotions. Then he added pensively, "We can give you all kinds of medications, even do surgical procedures on your heart. But you may want to understand what has been going on in your life that made your heart so vulnerable."

Now a forty-two-year-old Latina with a bright smile and cautious eyes, Christina leaned toward me apologetically. "I really don't know why I am here," she confessed. "My life is fine today. I have my daughter and husband and my work as an educator, teaching immigrant children. I should be over my past."

I replied, "Those hurts from the past are deep inside your body and psyche and need careful understanding and care." I explained that through mindfulness and compassion practices, I could support her in cultivating relevant and accessible ways to heal her wounded heart and to find ease within herself and with others.

Slowly and carefully, Christina began to unearth the memories of her early years. She began to understand and feel tenderly toward the little girl she had been. She came to realize that, unknowingly, she had felt guilty for not having been able to save her mother's life and, as a consequence, how she had actually been feeling alienated from her own emotions and needs.

Seeing that Christina was burdened by a deep-seated sense of shame and self-loathing, I suggested loving awareness and self-compassion practices. I began our visits with mindfulness meditation, which allowed her to be calm and awake in the present moment. The quietness of the meditation gives us the opportunity to tap into a benevolent field of awareness within and around us. As part of this meditation, I added the Heart's Intention Practice (which is introduced in Chapter 9) because it connects us to what is meaningful in our own lives as well as to the deep wish for the well-being of all.

With a foundation of mindful awareness and supported by the focus of the Heart's Intention Practice, we began to create phrases of self-compassion that felt true to Christina's feelings:

- May I extend understanding and warmth toward myself, as I feel so afraid and wounded.
- May I gently contain the worry that I will lose my home and those I love again.
- May I offer compassion toward myself so feelings of self-blame and unworthiness can soften.
- May I forgive myself and those who hurt me in the past.
- May I include all those who are suffering in this world in my compassion.
- May we all find peace in our hearts again.

Over time, the repetition of these phrases helped Christina to lean into her pain. It allowed her to tolerate her vulnerability and thus restore her inner balance.

As a psychotherapist and a Buddhist meditator, I have developed compassion practices such as this one over many years—both for my own benefit in facing my painful life challenges and also to help my clients and students. This approach of using phrases to cultivate balance developed out of the Buddha's teachings on the immeasurable virtues: loving-kindness, compassion, sympathetic joy, and equanimity. These are ancient psychological practices with the intention of planting seeds to cultivate our hearts.

Although these practices are often thought of as being primarily oriented toward others, they necessarily begin with developing our capacity to be kind and compassionate toward ourselves. Self-compassion allows us to take a look at our reactions, thoughts, and emotions with kindness and honesty, and it makes it possible for us to stay with our hurts; it is only when we recognize and feel our wounds that we can begin to free ourselves of them. Then it is possible to open our hearts to others.

Fifteen years ago, I went through a divorce. I felt dreadfully scared, worried about the welfare of my then-small children, terrified about the state of my finances, and anxious about losing my circle of friends. In fact, at times I felt completely panicked, sitting up in bed at night and unable to sleep because I was so worried about the future. Recognizing the stress my kids were experiencing, I ended up criticizing myself. Harsh thoughts circled endlessly through my mind: *Couldn't I have prevented this breakup? Why didn't I avert this pain from flooding our family?*

Realizing how stressed I was during this painful time of separation, I decided to restore my equilibrium by recommitting myself to a dedicated meditation practice. I had learned meditation from a Buddhist monk in Sri Lanka when I was twenty-three, but while my three children were small, my practice had become sporadic.

Now I decided to practice daily again and commit to attending two weeklong silent retreats per year. On retreat, when spending my days meditating quietly in a safe place, I was able to relax, regain my focus, and reconnect with my meditation teachers. Retreat time helped me to widen my perspective, and I was able to see what was valuable and true beyond my clouded perceptions. Yet I knew I couldn't sustain this broad perspective when I returned home. I needed further practices that addressed my habit of self-blame; I needed practices that would heal my bruised heart.

As I learned through my own journey, when you meet your suffering, your path becomes one of healing. However, it is only when you lean into your pain while holding yourself with tenderness that the wound itself can become a portal to transformation. The Buddha talked about compassion as "tenderness of heart." With both compassion and mindfulness practice, your heart and mind can gradually soften and open to life. The meditations and practices presented in this book will give you a path to walk with loving presence and an approach to help guide your efforts.

In developing these practices, I drew on the knowledge I learned from my Buddhist teachers, from Western psychological research, and from my own life experiences. Early Buddhist teachings arose in the simplicity and structure of monasteries. Ordinary people in today's world crave direct experience of the sacred in their lives and long for practices that allow them to access inner happiness and live life with equanimity and compassion.

While attempting to cope with the snowballing stresses in our contemporary world, you may notice yourself detaching from others, from your community, and from political and environmental concerns. This increasing sense of separation and anonymity can lead to fear and alienation in what feels like an uncaring and unsafe environment. This "trance of separation," as Buddhist teacher Tara Brach calls it, leads to an endemic perception of not being good enough. You may be experiencing this feeling in your own life, which leads to a sense of self-criticism. It can make you feel that you are not capable of getting everything done or that you fear you will not do things well enough. Fear is often at the root of your wounded heart: it might be the fear of blatant danger; the fear of what happens when the known comes to an end; or the fear of not being validated, included, or loved. Fear makes you contract—turn against yourself and others—which can then lead to frustration, guilt, and shame. A zeitgeist of competitiveness and fear reinforces the pain you may be experiencing on an individual level. Rather than exercising self-compassion, you may be habitually cold and critical toward yourself; rather than having compassion for others, you may sometimes feel blaming and intolerant. You may then feel confused about how to develop such virtues as loving-kindness and compassion. I call such pandemic contraction an "Ice Age of the heart."

These days I am a working mother with three young adult children; a full practice as psychotherapist and meditation teacher; and a husband, two dogs, and one cat. As I continue to work with my clients and students, such as Christina, I understand that people need a path that is available and helpful in dealing with the particulars of daily life. Even though weeklong retreats are wonderful and reflect a more traditional way of following the path of mindfulness and compassion, I recognize that I need to find practices that allow me and other working mothers and fathers, as well as busy single folks, to bring mindfulness and kindhearted concern into the situations that come up every day.

My husband, Michael, is a hospice doctor who works with people who are dying and with their grief-stricken families. During the past fifteen years, he has been studying nature-based Native American spiritual practices, which he incorporates into his work with those at the end of life. Michael and I have had many valuable debates. Our ongoing conversations have challenged me to develop an approach that finds a balance between compassion for oneself and compassion for the world.

My conversations with Michael often return to the teachings of interconnectedness, which means an understanding that all things "inter-are." We both see interconnectedness as fundamental to the way we understand the nature of reality. We agree that insight into interconnectedness leads naturally to a deep feeling of responsibility and caring. In my work I always set an intention for the well-being of all. Nonetheless, I tend to begin with self-compassion, while Michael tends to begin with compassion for all life.

On one of our ritual evening walks, he once looked at me intently and said, "I am worried that our need for self-compassion is endless and gets stuck in our own desires before it is ready to move out into the first sweep of the spiral." Michael imagines compassion as extending from our hearts in a spiral-like, outward motion to include more and more of the world around us. He added, "Whatever we're doing about self-compassion, we can't wait hoping that it will spread to the outer sweep of the spiral all by itself."

I countered by stating the reverse perspective: "But caring engagement for others and our world without self-compassion is a recipe for depletion and burnout. We need 'both-and'—we need to develop self-compassion while simultaneously developing awareness of the outer arc of the spiral. We need to attend to the outer sweep while genuinely caring for ourselves."

In working with Christina, I have found this balance between compassion and self-compassion. I regard it as crucial to generate practices that bring compassion to both the civil war in Argentine society and, at the same time, to Christina's suffering in her own heart. Individuals like Christina exist in all societies and ecosystems of this world. Argentina might be seen as a metaphor for the many places of war, unrest, and danger. As you engage with *Heartwork*, you will find a dynamic interplay between the emphasis on compassion for yourself and compassion for all. In fact, the practices of mindfulness meditation, self-compassion, and compassion for all are interconnected.

Through mindfulness meditation, you connect to the all-pervasive benevolent field, and with your practice of intention for the well-being of all, you connect to the world. As your wounded heart begins to heal with self-compassion, it naturally begins to fill with generosity and kindness; the boundaries of your self-preoccupation begin to loosen, and compassion for yourself widens to embrace compassion for all life.

This is a book about meditations and practices that allow you to cultivate compassion for yourself, others, and your world. *Heartwork* has three sections. In Part I, I relate my own story. My passion for finding healing through compassion practices evolved from extremely painful times in my life, such as being hidden for two years in an orphanage, growing up without a father, and overcoming the judgments of a disparaging Catholic family. My destiny began to turn around when I looked into the wise, eternal eyes of Damaloka, an ancient monk in Sri Lanka. Diligent spiritual practice paired with the wisdom of psychotherapy has continued to teach me that it is possible to transform suffering into happiness. The miraculous can happen.

The process of writing about my experiences, my turning points, as well as what I have learned, has been invaluable to me in the ongoing process of healing wounds and finding self-compassion and compassion for all. At the end of each chapter, I include a few journal prompts with which I invite you to write freely about your own experiences, turning points, and lessons you've learned.

In Part II, I share nine practices that help you to cultivate compassion. I present formal meditations that will teach you the art of mindfulness and how to treat your heart with loving awareness. You learn how to set a heart's intention so that your efforts will have power and direction. I teach practices for self-compassion that can help you transform a critical stance you have taken toward yourself into a solid friendship you can build with yourself. Self-compassion allows your heart to heal and lets you include others in your care. As the spiral widens, you learn to align yourself with the guiding force of *bodhichitta*, or "the heart that cares for all," which is the deep desire for the well-being and happiness of all beings, including yourself. This will allow you to tap into the energy of the universe and guide you to develop compassion for all life. Focusing on the spiral of compassion and forgiveness brings compassion, mercy, and acceptance to hurt relationships.

I also offer short practices for life "on the go." In these Mindfulness On-the-Go practices, I provide brief phrases that can help you pause, slow down, and ground yourself in self-compassion so that you can reengage in more skillful and balanced ways with the challenges of life. The goal is to make these on-the-go practices relevant and accessible during stressful, painful, or perplexing life events so you can bring an attitude of caring and awareness into the heart of your daily life. Each chapter in Part II is followed by key points, a sample practice, and journal prompts.

In Part III, I present stories of people who grapple with the same challenges many of us face and who use these meditation and compassion practices to cultivate emotional balance and peace. I hope these stories give you a chance to see how you can bring these practices to your own problems, especially if you are facing anxiety and fear or have experienced abandonment, rejection, or loss. It is my hope that when your health is fragile or when you are plagued by self-criticism, shame, or guilt, you will recognize your own experience in these stories.

I will also show you how painful behavior patterns that may have been passed down through generations can slowly be transformed to change your life's direction. Self-compassion, even though fundamental to this transformation, is not an end in itself; instead, it gives you the foundation for opening yourself to the world with compassion and love.

When you want others to be happy, practice compassion;
if you want to be happy, practice compassion.

—The Dalai Lama

HOW TO USE THIS BOOK

Inspirational in the many stories that illustrate the practices presented, *Heartwork* can be approached in a variety of ways, depending on your needs. To experience the full richness of the book, you may want to read it from beginning to end so you can draw encouragement from the stories while learning step-by-step the full range of skills I suggest for working with compassion. Or you may gravitate to a particular practice that you know you want to learn, such as mindfulness or self-compassion, or to particular themes that reflect your current struggles and aspirations, such as family pain, work stress, or money problems.

In *Heartwork*, you will find stories from my own life and from the lives of my psychotherapy clients and meditation students. Through these stories, you have a chance to reach out and connect emotionally with others while at the same time learning something about yourself and broadening your possibilities. Life is full of stories—from the story of getting to work in the morning to the story of a relationship breakup. All of us deal with struggles and challenges every day of our lives. Those are the stories presented here, and I hope that you will make them your own.

When I tell my story in Part I, you will get to know me as a person who walks the path of vulnerability. You will learn how through mistakes and experiments, heartache and moments of connection and joy, I developed the practices I am offering you. From a beginning in a German orphanage, I encountered Buddhist wisdom in Sri Lanka at the age of twenty-three when I looked into the eyes of an old monk. As a wife, mother, and young professional, compassion meditations became my own medicine, which I now pass on. The journal prompts at the end of each chapter will help you make a bridge to your own heart.

In Part II, I share many practices that will help you cultivate compassion, such as the Self-Compassion Practice, the Spiral of Compassion and Forgiveness Practice, and the Loving Awareness Practice. These practices will help you heal feelings of hurt and alienation by nurturing compassion, acceptance, and forgiveness for others and yourself. All practices are summarized in boxes. I teach you to bring the guiding phrases and meditations to your life challenges, especially when facing anxiety, fear, rejection, or loss. The Compassionate Choice Practice chart and worksheet will help you to clearly recognize your reactivity, to slow down, and to respond more skillfully in challenging moments. A website with worksheets and various practices/cards (Mindfulpause.org) will complement your understanding.

Key points at the end of each chapter will help you to integrate and deepen what you have learned. I suggest allowing yourself to "free write," letting the story and key points awaken in you a sense of reflection about your own experiences. Engaging with the Journal Exercises will help deepen and nourish your own heartwork.

In Part III, I present stories of people from a variety of countries, ethnicities, religious, and sexual backgrounds who use compassion practices to cultivate emotional balance and peace. Each of the stories should spur you to bring and adapt the practices to your own life. For example, Gregory's Mindful Pause and Compassionate Choice practices save him from destroying his life with his violent temper. Loraine learns to love and accept all aspects of herself during the process of transitioning from a male to a female body. Heidi's self-compassion practices heal her transgenerational wounds of immigration, poverty, and marginalization. Again, there are journal prompts at the end of each chapter.

Witnessing how the story protagonists integrate the recommended practices effectively may help you to imagine how your life could unfold in new and healing ways. Alongside the everyday heroines and heroes described in *Heartwork*, you will learn how to relate with love and compassion. When expressing warmth and caring becomes your spontaneous response, you will find yourself living with increased happiness, generosity, and ease. The stories are intended not only to provide inspiration but to encourage a sense of confidence in your own capacity to work with your life circumstances in alignment with your heart's intention.

PART ONE

My Story

Waking Up

On a September day in 1980 during the monsoon season, I walked by myself in the pouring rain down a road in Colombo, Sri Lanka. Accompanied by my boyfriend, Hans, I had come as a young German student to recover from two serious car accidents, eight weeks in the hospital, and the traumas of traditional Western medical training. As I walked down the noisy road lined with vendors offering their colorful goods, I breathed in the steamy dampness. A street sign that read International Buddhist Center Road caught my eye. Spurred only by intuition, I entered a narrow alleyway leading to a large stone building. Having no idea what to expect, I rang a heavy doorbell. A slender young monk in yellow robes opened the door.

"What do you want?" he asked in pigeon English.

Bewildered, I answered, "I don't know."

"Very good," he said with a smile and an inviting gesture. "Follow me."

Up and down stairs and through corridors we went, deeper and deeper into the belly of a monastery. Finally we ended up in a spacious, darkened room in the depths of this surprisingly big building. A number of solemn, senior monks in ochre robes were sitting on dark cushions. My young guide stopped in front of the most ancient-looking monk. In fact, this old man, who was sitting with his eyes closed, looked to me like a mummy. He was tiny, all skin and bones, almost drowning in the bounty of his robes. Taking me by surprise, the ancient monk opened his eyes and looked straight through me.

I had never experienced something like that. The monk's face expressed understanding and compassion, the quality of which seemed different from anything I had ever seen in a person before. His kind eyes were calm, clear, and completely alive. I was amazed to feel as if I were downright transparent, as if the monk could see everything about me. Dazed, I did not think at all. I was just in that moment.

"What do you want?" the ancient monk asked.

I repeated what I had said to the first monk, "I don't know." Then, hesitantly, almost apologetically, I added, "I want to learn."

"Very good," the old monk responded. Then he nodded his head thoughtfully and said, "Come back every morning at 9:15 A.M."

And that is what I did for the next three weeks, the remainder of my time in Colombo, while Hans studied acupuncture. I still remember the musty smell in that huge basement room; the shadows of the monks sitting in complete quiet; and the pervasive, all-encompassing silence. Through the meetings with the ancient monk—whose name, I found out later, was Damaloka—I was introduced to a timeless, formless way of being, beyond my mundane, worldly concerns. Even though I could not explain what was happening, I was hooked. Having been accustomed to harshness and disapproval from my family, Damaloka's compassionate acceptance was both soothing and liberating. My inner disquiet and fear dissolved. Slowly my heart, and even my tormented mind, started to relax. I was surprised that I could sit in stillness without discomfort. A sense of ease swept through my body, and I felt as if I had come home.

From that first meeting on, I found that I did not want to leave when the old monk hinted that our little lessons were over. When I left the monastery at noon, the rain had stopped pouring down on the pavement, and the sun had come out. I felt much lighter around my heart. When I joined the crowds of people walking down the buzzing and colorful streets of Colombo, I didn't know what I had encountered on the small round cushion, but I did know that I wanted more of whatever it was: I might call it translucent wisdom, or unconditional peace and compassion.

One day Hans and I met the famous scholar and monk, Nyanaponika Thera, who ended up sending us to Black Rock Hermitage, a small Buddhist retreat center deep in the forest and far away from any village. Bante Kashepa, a scholarly and kind young monk, was the Vipassana teacher there. He patiently taught us how to sit quietly for at least eight hours a day. He instructed us on basic mindfulness, how to watch our thoughts and feelings, and how to learn about the workings of our minds as well as the qualities of our hearts. Learning to turn my gaze inward and look straight into the landscape of difficult emotions felt greatly empowering to me. Meditation had allowed me to slowly sink beneath the fog of my inner restlessness, angst, and confusion and to touch the ground of peacefulness. At the hermitage, the teaching from Nyanaponika's famous book, *The Heart of Buddhist Meditation*, became the foundation for my practice. I sometimes joke that if our visas had not expired, we might still be sitting there, meditating with Bante Kashepa at Black Rock Hermitage.

Sitting beside the trail leading from my hut to the temple, I remember being mesmerized by watching a column of ants crossing the path. Being perfectly mindful and in the present moment, I admired their purposeful movements and how each one, just like me, had its perfect place. I experienced the ants and myself as constantly changing, as being part of the whole, huge everything. I felt so much love for those ants and all that was around me. Finally, I had found a loving refuge inside my own mind and heart.

These first spiritual experiences in Sri Lanka came as a surprise to me. Having been a German medical student steeped in the world of science, I knew almost nothing about Buddhism or meditation. I just knew that I was hurting from the struggles in my life and from not knowing how to go on. When I sat down on the little round cushion, I did not know if I would encounter an existential black hole or experience myself as a meaningless speck in an equally meaningless universe. Instead I felt a deep sense of calm, tranquility, and ease. While meditating, I did not encounter an alienated, frightening universe, as portrayed by the world I had grown up in with my family. What emerged were love, compassion, gratitude, and most of all peace as the ground of being.

Through the serious car accidents, which I had barely survived, I had come to a crossroads. The direct experience of the sacred through deep meditation allowed me to have personal knowledge of the love and wisdom that is primordially there inside all of us when we become very still. Years later I heard a Buddhist teacher say, "For the miraculous to happen is an accident. But practice makes us accident-prone." That statement captured my experience. Now I know that this understanding and practice are open to everyone who allows for the right conditions to occur.

After leaving Sri Lanka, Hans wanted to visit Herakhan, a small Shiva ashram in the foothills of the Himalayas. So once again, we took off for the unknown. Departing from the last tiny village our rickety bus could reach in Uttar Pradesh, we trekked for eight hours through rivers and over mountains until we found the ashram. Surrounded by high mountains, Herakhan lay perched along the beginnings of the river Ganges. This colorful ashram, decorated with murals of the gods and wildflowers all around, was different from the Buddhist monastery, which had been beautiful but in a stark and serene sort of way. The Buddhist meditation method was one of emptying out, of absolute simplicity. In silent meditation, we had learned to release everything that distracts us so that we could experience reality as it is.

The Hindu path offered a startling contrast that showed me there are different ways to have a deep and authentic spiritual experience. I wept with the music, the sounds of *aratis* and *kirtanas*, as my heart opened. I carried stones during Karma Yoga and helped build walls for the ashram garden. This was the path of experiencing the sacred through love and devotion.

In Herakhan I realized that I could surrender to love itself, love for everything, and that love would dispel fear. I learned that my way of showing this love could be through my work. All work could be done out of love for God, out of love for everything alive.

After returning from my long trip through Sri Lanka and India, I longed to ground my life in the deep, unfathomable mystery as well as in tenderness and compassion. Spiritual practice became the path I began to trust; it eventually opened closed doors and allowed insight and kindness to pour in.

As my path unfolded, the Buddhist approach of emptying out, of looking inward with kind discipline, and the Hindu path of love and unity began to flow together. In an interwoven, mutually supportive way, they united as the path of compassion, interdependence, and love.

JOURNAL EXERCISE

My story may have brought up memories from your own time growing up and the turning points in your life. Sit down with a pencil and paper in a quiet place. Make yourself comfortable, rest in your gentle breath, and see what images and stories arise as you read the following prompts. If your own experiences come to mind, do some "free writing." This is a technique in which you write continuously for a set period of time without regard for spelling, grammar, or topic. Writing freely may help you overcome blocks of apathy and self-criticism.

1. In your younger years, did you encounter spiritual, numinous, or profound compassion? If so, when and where did these experiences occur? How did they make you feel?
2. Were there guides who helped you on your path? Who were they, and how did they inspire you?
3. Think back to a moment when you were at a crossroads. Is there anything that you wish you had known at the time? What have you learned about your journey since then? Write a letter to yourself at a moment when you were experiencing a difficult transition or a period of uncertainty.

Transformation of Suffering

The only memory I have of my father is the story my mother told me when I was six years old. The narrative goes that on a chilly Bavarian late afternoon in the fall of 1957, she took me to a prearranged meeting place with the goal of introducing me, the infant, to him, the father. We arrived to find a piece of torn-off brown paper with a note: "I do not want to see the child."

My mother and father met when they were both doctors working for a lung sanatorium situated in one of the most remote regions of the Bavarian mountains. An unexpected pregnancy split the new relationship apart. Whenever I heard or remembered that story, I felt a gashing tear in my heart.

My mother hid her condition from her relatives and even from her fellow doctors. Haunted by the judgment of her family, she quit work and closeted herself in a secret hideaway until the time of delivery. A faded black-and-white photo shows me at age one in an orphanage, a place where my mother kept me hidden from her stern Catholic relatives. One of many children in a row of little beds, I was standing in a tiny white crib, holding on to the bars with my small hands. My eyes were glazed over and tuned out.

When I was about two, my mother finally introduced me to her family, pretending that I was an adopted child. Fear of criticism and judgment from her family had led my mother to concoct this tale, which would cause me much shame later in life. Those early experiences left me with a fear that I would never be accepted and loved, as well as a strong longing for a life that was more just and caring then the one I had been dealt. A deep, nagging anxiety and a sense of being unsure of myself set the foundation for my work teaching self-compassion.

I have wondered why I have so many clients and students who have experienced early abandonment and loss, accompanied by shame and fear. I have discovered that our capacity for having an open and caring heart is as great as the suffering we have experienced.

The aftermath of the two world wars had left the members of my family traumatized in a twilight world of uncertainty and secrets, at odds with each other and the world. Everyone I knew was a refugee and had lost possessions, relatives, pride, confidence, and self-respect in those far-away regions of Eastern Europe. It was common at the time for inter-twined collective and personal trauma to be passed down through generations of families, leaving children bewildered and without a secure emotional place.

The members of our family were constantly at war with one another and the world around them. Like a little soldier, I would sneak from one hostile camp within our family to another, trying to keep peace among the parties. The stress took its toll on my little seven-year-old body. I developed tuberculosis and suffered from heart trouble. I remember the huge heart monitor I had to carry around in a big black box.

Yet looking back, I realize that amid the darkness, there was also light. Over the years I encountered key mentors whose example helped me to wake up and experience the power of love and fierce compassion. My grandfather, a doctor of philosophy, was one of my heroes. As a teacher, he had spoken out during the early days of Nazism, informing his pupils about the lawlessness of the National Socialist Party. His outspokenness had cost him his job and caused him to be condemned to a labor camp. My grandmother, his wife, a fierce little woman standing four foot two, pushed a Nazi officer down the stairs after he had repeatedly forced his way in to search their apartment. I was raised on stories of Auschwitz, where my mother, a medic, nursed those who had survived the horrors of the Nazi regime as the war ended. Her courage to face her own fear and her dedication to tend to those in need reinforced my commitment to a life dedicated to compassionate action.

As I look back on it, service may have saved my life. Coming from this particularly anguished situation, where my place in the family was so uncertain, in a country whose cultural and moral fabric was in great disarray, service to others became my touchstone. I worked in my mother's clinic, and from age seventeen on, I worked as a substitute on a hospice unit. I remember the eighty-four-year-old Frau Elstner sitting in her bed wearing a light blue jacket. Secretly I helped her deliver letters to a girlfriend, whose relatives had placed her in a different home. Serving Frau Elstner and the other old ladies helped me to truly learn to love.

I felt enormous pressure from my family to study medicine and take over my mother's clinic. But I was increasingly frustrated by how much emphasis was given to the technical, pharmaceutical, and business aspects of the medical field. Fate must have noticed me and put a stop to my faltering attempts to please my tribe. Two major car accidents within three months caused serious trauma to my head and neck and left my forehead badly scarred.

I reached a turning point in the hospital. I was afraid that I would die if I did not change my life. I was freed to rethink what really mattered to me, which prompted me to start following my own path of searching for what is meaningful and life-giving. This was when I took a leave of absence from medical school and went to Sri Lanka with the goal of studying acupuncture as an adjunct to medicine. But my path took a different turn.

JOURNAL EXERCISE

Sit down with a pencil and paper in a quiet place. Make yourself comfortable, rest in your gentle breath, and see what images and stories arise as you read the following prompts. Please do some free writing about your experiences.

1. With a compassionate heart, think of your early life, the beautiful and the hurtful times. Can you isolate a specific painful episode to write about? Remember through all of your senses what kind of suffering there was—loss, abandonment, abuse, disappointment, shame, fear, sadness, or anger.

2. Describe some landmarks in your young life and turnings toward insight and compassion. No matter how small or fleeting the experience, bring as much detail as you can to mind. Take a moment to stay with these memories.

3. Think about the role of your community in these incidents, both in terms of contributing to your suffering or, alternatively, in helping you heal. This is a big question. In particular, was there someone you recall helping at the time or who you realize now was trying to be of help? How does it feel remembering him or her now?

3

Waking Up in Daily Life

In my beginning explorations of the Buddhist teachings, I was in danger of sidestepping the deep emotional wounds I had received during my childhood by leaping headlong into spiritual ideas. Like many others, I used spiritual practice to bypass feelings of vulnerability and fear. Unknowingly, I avoided experiencing what writer John Welwood calls, "the nakedness and openness, which arise when we are open to face the imperfections of our human existence."[1]

A brief marriage to an American man I met in India in 1983 brought me to the United States. After we separated, I sought out a series of wise, compassionate, and skillful psychotherapists, who helped me to understand my background as well as how to build a foundation for this next phase of my life.

The path of personal development through psychotherapy allowed me to experience my feelings deeply and to understand the enormity of my fear, grief, anger, and self-doubt. Within the sheltered environment and with the "positive regard" of each therapist, I was able to begin to explore and express my tender emotions safely. For the first time, I experienced heartfelt caring for the particular distress and sorrow I had suffered.

Through the compassionate eyes of my therapists, I learned to develop empathy for myself as a vulnerable and wounded person.

Complementing the psychological path, spiritual practice gave me a glimpse of hope that it was possible to find a sense of ease. Mindfulness meditation gave me confidence in my ability to work with my mind. I learned that I could cultivate inner tranquility and a heightened sense of being present and aware in a constantly changing world. I also found that through meditation I was able to work with my heart, so that I could discern genuine feelings and emotional nuances and, underneath those, a deep intuitive sense of knowing. I also discovered that, beneath the enormous suffering that exists in our world, the basic structure of life is benevolent and wise.

When I had lived in Santa Barbara for just a few months, I met the psychoanalyst and spiritual seeker Benjamin Weininger. Ben led me to what I have come to see as a most adept level of psychotherapy, one that is saturated with deep spiritual understanding.

Through Ben, I became exposed to some of the spiritual visionaries of our time, such as Krishnamurti, Houston Smith, Ram Dass, David Bohm, and a multitude of Tibetan monks. My world in Germany had been small, and the trauma of the past had led to a narrow understanding of life. Ben and his spiritual philosopher friends gave me permission and encouragement to reimagine for myself what is truly meaningful in life and what would bring healing to my and others' frightened and wounded hearts.

Ben was also one of the first Jewish men I had ever known. I was touched that a Jewish family invited me, a German girl, into their house. I first knew Ben as a teacher, but later, after I met and fell in love with his son Reuben, Ben became my father-in-law.

On New Year's Eve 1991, twelve years after I had been introduced to serious meditation practice in Sri Lanka and four years after coming to California, I had a child with Reuben. Soon two more children followed. Even though we deeply loved and enjoyed our little ones, the practical affairs of life, such as attending to several small children as well as marriage and work, were not easy for me to juggle. I was thrown into a profound depression. It took me many years to feel I had untied the most painful knots that originated from my reemerging childhood wounds. After fourteen years, Reuben and I separated. I had several years of confusion, loneliness, and distress about how to find my balance again and how to provide a protected and happy life for my three children. Besides reclaiming a safe place in the office of a good psychotherapist, I needed the diligence and daring of meditation practice to face my worries and fears. In the midst of those painful years, I stepped up my meditation practice, attended retreats, and reconnected with my main spiritual teacher, Jack Kornfield.

However, I realized that I had to find a way to incorporate what I had learned in meditation practice into ordinary life. This process felt like slowly kneading air, salt, and spice into a thick slab of dough. For my own sake, and that of my clients, I had to find a way to bridge the gap between formal meditation "on the cushion" and mindfulness in daily life or "on the go," especially when life became increasingly stressful.

At the same time, I discovered that the painful experience of divorce and of learning how to forgive those I felt had hurt me throughout my life actually gave me the foundation for developing practices for compassion and forgiveness. Over time, learning to be aware and caring even in the midst of great hurt and disappointment became a form of practice for me.

Then I met Michael, a hospice doctor in Dublin, Ireland, who transformed my life; we married in 2005. From Michael and our mentor, Joanna Macy, I also learned about *bodhichitta*, the deep wish to wake up spiritually and psychologically for the sake of all beings. Bodhichitta, which may be interpreted as "the heart that cares for all," teaches you that your work for the well-being of all beings (including the environment) is the highest aspiration you can hold and far more important than a focus on your individual comfort. The aspiration of bodhichitta began to nourish my practice. Over the past fifteen years, Michael and I have based our work together in training doctors and other health professionals on the principle of bodhichitta; it is the foundation for the compassion training presented in this book.

JOURNAL EXERCISE

Sit down with a pencil and paper in a quiet place. Make yourself comfortable, rest in your gentle breath, and see what images and stories arise as you read the following prompts. If your own experiences come to mind, do some free writing.

1. Write about a time when you grappled with the imperfections and seeming unfairness of life. What did you learn?
2. Write about a time when there was a conflict in your heart between what you felt you "should" do to satisfy the norms of society and your own intuition.
3. Write about a time when you have struggled to balance everyday life and a spiritual practice. What, if anything, has helped you regain balance?

4

Finding the Heart

Through all the years of training, finding a profession, marrying, having kids, and even twenty some years of undergoing classical psychotherapy and psychoanalysis, I still often suffered from feeling that I was not good enough, unlovable, and ultimately deeply alone. When I learned that kindness and compassion for myself were possible, it was completely revolutionary for me.

Sharon Salzberg's 2002 book on loving-kindness, *Lovingkindness*, was groundbreaking for Western meditators who were trying to bring our practice into daily life while frantically striving to manage our relationships and/or children as well as competitive work environments. The need to pair a wisdom practice—mindfulness—with a heart practice became blatantly evident to me.

"May I be happy, may I be free, may I live with ease" were the phrases that would become meaningful for me while trying to steady frantic professional and personal lives with a spiritual one. Buddhism teaches four fundamental positive qualities of being, or the "four immeasurables." These heart qualities help you to develop love or loving-kindness, which is the wish for others to be happy; compassion, the wish that others will be free from suffering; joy, the sense of delight when others are happy and free from suffering; and equanimity, which is the yearning to cultivate these wishes toward an immeasurable number of sentient beings. As thought-feelings, they open your heart toward yourself and others. The four immeasurables can be cultivated through steady practice, and they complement mindfulness. While the effect of mindfulness practice is a calming of the mind, leaving you more peaceful and present, cultivating the four immeasurables allows you to become loving, caring, and joyful in a balanced and wise way.

As they are often mentioned together in one breath, I would like to contrast loving-kindness and compassion practices. Even though both practices cultivate your heart, they have different qualities. Loving-kindness practice increases your ability to wish others well and to think of them kindly. Wishing for another person to be healthy, happy, and safe is a huge step from feeling disparaging, dismissive, or even just plain neutral toward him or her. With loving-kindness, you begin to open your heart to the other person so he or she can begin to matter to you.

When I first practiced loving-kindness, I had a difficult neighbor toward whom I wanted to develop a friendlier attitude. I created the following loving-kindness phrases:

- May my heart be full of loving-kindness.
- May I meet you with friendship and peace.
- May you be happy and live with ease.
- May you be free.

Compassion practice asks you to open your heart on a deep and profound level and allows you "to feel with" your own as well as another's suffering. Compassion practice spoke to me because of the pain I encountered on the curvy path of my life.

Compassion for myself allowed me to meet the worries and doubts of my heart. The most important aspect here is "to feel with." American Indians call this willingness to experience what it feels like in another person's body and heart, "to walk in another's moccasins." Implicit here is the willingness to sense someone else's suffering, which implies that you yourself are willing to move out of your comfort zone. Many of you may first need to feel your own pain and learn to walk with compassion in your own shoes. As your heart opens in this way, you have the energy to include others in your caring.

When a friend's daughter had an accident that reminded me of the accidents I had suffered as a young adult, I developed the following compassion phrases:

- May I offer you compassion in this time of hurt.
- May I extend my tender care toward you as you face great vulnerability.
- May you be free from suffering and the causes of suffering.
- May you again live your life with ease.

When I began to experiment with compassion practices, I found that I became engaged when they had a meaningful flavor for me. During the early years of going on retreat, I had started to build loving-kindness into my practice. Yet as hard as I tried, I often was not able to *feel* the phrases in my heart. On the other hand, compassion allowed me to feel deeply with myself, even when what I discovered in myself was uncomfortable and painful to look at. This profound self-caring allowed me to turn even distressing experiences into spiritual learning. I was surprised to find that compassion meditation was not as widely used as loving-kindness practice, and I became interested in helping to change that.

Jack Kornfield was the first one to introduce me to loving-kindness and compassion practice. He was able to recognize and understand me in a *personal way* in my own, at times painful, circumstances as well as in a *spiritual way* as someone who recognizes the vastness of ultimate reality. When the personal, sometimes frightened aspects of myself were appreciated, I found I could relax a little and let go into a universal perspective.

I remember the day when Jack first taught me to develop compassion for myself. It was on a November retreat ten or twelve years ago at Spirit Rock Meditation Center in Marin County, California. The day was gray, freezing cold, and damp when he gave me the task of devoting a full ten-day retreat, morning to night, to loving-kindness and compassion—beginning with myself. In a profound way, he encouraged me to embrace my anguish and visit the deepest places of my misery while regarding them as aspects of spiritual practice. From this experience grew my understanding of how compassion practices can become a psychospiritual path, a path that can help us in psychological as well as spiritual ways. My hope is that such understanding can assist me to help others who are also in pain.

JOURNAL EXERCISE

Sit down with a pencil and paper in a quiet place. Make yourself comfortable, rest in your gentle breath, and see what images and stories arise as you read the following prompts. If your own experiences come to mind, do some free writing.

1. What is your relationship to your own heart, the organ of psychological and spiritual perception, of intuition and the longing to connect? Can you remember a particular time in your life when you discovered your relationship to your heart?
2. Write about a time in your life when you felt disconnected from yourself, when it was hard for you to experience compassion and warmth for yourself.
3. Think about someone for whom you had (or have) difficulty feeling loving-kindness and/or compassion. In your heart, see if you can feel the difference between offering loving-kindness and offering compassion.

5

The Birth of
My Compassion Practice

When I entered the retreat center's dining hall on a rainy afternoon in 2008, my heart skipped a beat. I saw three women with whom I'd had a difficult time almost twenty years earlier. They were sitting huddled together around one of the long gray tables. We were about to start a four-week silent retreat together. I looked away and quickly went to sit down at one of the faraway tables, feeling a sense of doom about the prospect of spending twenty-eight days of silent retreat with people by whom I had felt so deeply rejected. I have come to see the story of this retreat as a breakthrough in my understanding and creative use of compassion meditations.

Twenty years earlier, when I lived in Oakland, I was part of an intimate book group that consisted of eight women reading Buddhist books together. Some of us knew each other already from a birth group, and there had been a feeling of coziness and friendship. We took turns bringing dinner to our book group and talked about raw and important issues in our lives. Over time, though, conflicts began to emerge. Some of us wanted to read books from a specific Buddhist tradition in order to sink more deeply into that particular philosophy. I was in a minority of women who wanted to read a variety of books from different Buddhist traditions as well as other religious backgrounds in order to explore key themes that seemed relevant to the sufferings of modern life.

As time went on, the rift came to a head. One day the three ringleaders of the traditionally inclined faction invited me for tea. Not knowing what this was about, I was excited to exchange ideas. However, when we sat down together, the three told me in no uncertain terms that I had to leave the group. My "diffuse" interests threatened to "destroy" their fundamental purpose. They had no interest in talking this through, and the meeting ended abruptly. I was devastated by the rejection from these women with whom I had explored core values, hopes, and dreams and also shared the wonders of the birthing experience. I tried on several occasions to talk to them, hoping to find a bridge, but they refused to speak to me. Soon after I moved to Santa Barbara.

When I encountered those three women at the silent retreat, I was surprised by how fresh this old injury felt. But there I was, stuck for a month in the cauldron of this silent retreat with the people who had triggered such upset. During meditation, I found that much of my childhood grief and anxiety resurfaced, with a recurrent image of the little child in the orphanage standing alone with her eyes glazed over.

After about ten days of feeling like I was drowning in a deep black hole, I went to the community bookstore, where I found the Dalai Lama's little book *The Compassionate Life*. His Holiness said, "We must wait for difficulties to arise and then attempt to practice with them. And who creates such opportunities? Not our friends, of course, but our enemies." Those words assured me that the Dalai Lama could be my guide, allowing this difficult situation to become an asset on the path to learning to love.

Everything I had learned from years of practice began to integrate with these wonderful teachings from His Holiness. I began to build my own practice by developing meditations in compassion that were to benefit myself and others.

Self-compassion allowed me to sit quietly with the physical discomfort of aching legs and sore neck, while holding myself with gentleness and care. With gentle breathing, I was able to cool my inflamed mind and heart, and with gentle phrases, I was able to stay strong enough to tolerate the hurt and pain that had surfaced.

At the end of a long day of self-compassion and gentle breathing, I felt words of self-compassion rise up. My lips started to form the following phrases:

- May I hold myself with tenderness and care.
- May I offer compassion to my raw and wounded heart.
- May my wounds be healed.
- May I be free.

At first I felt merely numbness and a kind of coldness inside. Then the warmth of care and affection for myself began to thaw my frozen center. Gradually, my heart started to feel like a big aching wound. I murmured,

- May I be free from feelings of dread and hurt.
- May I be free from my own resentment and ill will.
- May I be free from anxiety and shame.
- May I be free to live and love fully.

The tightness around my heart loosened. Unexpectedly, after what seemed like a long time, the center area in my chest began to feel warm and tender, light and alive.

His Holiness's little book reminded me, "The moment you think only of yourself, the focus of your whole reality narrows and because of this narrow focus, uncomfortable things can appear huge and can bring you fear and discomfort and a sense of feeling overwhelmed by misery. The moment you think of others with a sense of caring, however, your view widens."[2]

Over the following days, images came up of countless other people to whom I wanted to extend my compassion. I saw my mother as a nineteen-year-old nurse staggering through the battlefields of World War II. I saw the young daughter of a friend, who was suffering from lymphoma, a cancer of the blood. Vividly in my mind's eye, I saw young soldiers in Gaza and Jerusalem, as well as teenage German soldiers from the terrible war in Europe seventy years earlier.

- May I offer support to those who experience war, poverty, and danger.
- May I extend warmth and care to all those who experience the wounds of violence, rejection, and fear.
- May we all be free.

Then the ripples kept moving outward naturally.

A feeling of compassion arose even for those by whom I felt rejected. Images of their three faces surfaced in my mind. I was beginning to sense the vulnerability underneath their seemingly tough shells. One day in the dining hall, one of the women had come over and put her hand on my shoulder for a moment as we passed each other. I remember her face softening and her beautifully patterned rose-colored scarf, which she had wrapped around her head and shoulders, seeming translucent in the early morning light. Later, the following phrases came to me as I imagined her standing there:

- May I extend my kindness and care also toward you, by whom I felt so hurt.
- May I be free to see your point of view, especially if it is different from mine.

Holding my pain with gentleness, yet at the same time reconnecting to a wiser, more universal ground, I prayed for our once intimate little book group:

- May wisdom and compassion give us the strength to be kind to each other.
- May we all have the courage to look at what is hard to face and go beyond.

- May we be free from suffering and the causes of suffering.
- May we all find the sustenance we need to live in peace.
- May life rise up to meet us all.

My heart yearned to expand so it could, for once, fully hold the pain of those other beings in this world who also struggle to survive and live; all creatures—humans, animals, the aching earth—began to surface as images in my mind. I imagined the geometry of compassion as an ever-widening spiral that would include more and more beings. Spontaneously the following prayer arose:

- May we understand that all of us are held by the field of benevolence.

After the retreat was over, this feeling of love and gratitude and the awareness of basic goodness did not stay with me in the same way. Over time my skin got thicker again, and my heart shrank back to its former size. But I have never quite forgotten that feeling of openness and the notion that, if everyone could experience a bit more of that openhearted feeling, the world would be a less harmful and a more compassionate place.

Inspired by this colorful, painful, and brilliantly fluid process, I decided to create practices to make what I had learned accessible and relevant to as many others as possible. I committed myself to using my skills as a psychologist and a meditation teacher to bring compassion practice from the cushion into all of our daily lives at times when we need it most. Through this experience, I received the template for the nine practices presented in this book that are intended to help cultivate a compassionate heart.

Sit down with a pencil and paper in a quiet place. Make yourself comfortable, rest in your gentle breath, and see what images and stories arise as you read the following prompts. If your own experiences come to mind, do some free writing.

1. Think about a time when you experienced grave disappointment or betrayal. Do some free writing about that experience and reflect on your feelings.
2. Have you ever experienced compassion and/or forgiveness that another person extended to you? Describe how that made you feel and what changed for you.
3. Were you ever able to offer compassion and/or forgiveness to someone who had hurt or angered you? Describe how that made you feel and how it changed your relationship to yourself and the other person.

PART TWO

Nine Practices for Cultivating Compassion

6

Introducing Nine Practices for Cultivating Compassion

It was thirty-five years ago that I looked into the eyes of the ancient monk in Colombo. I decided then that I would no longer be a victim to the painful themes in my life that recurred over and over again.

With psychotherapy and spiritual practice, I was willing to do whatever it took to free myself from old entanglements. Yet it took me many years—in fact, decades—to discover the practices needed for such transformation. Even more than developing philosophies and methods, it was crucial for me to develop the intention to care for myself with effective and intelligent practices.

Ancient Buddhist teachings and modern cognitive science and neuroscience assert that ways of thinking, feeling, and relating, as well as attitudes about life, can be cultivated with the help of relevant and accessible practices. Practicing mindfulness and compassion on an ongoing basis can lead to significant changes not only to your habits and attitudes but also in the workings of your heart and brain. The practices that I present to you in this book originate in ancient teachings. They are informed by my thirty-five years of meditation and thirty years of working with clients in my psychotherapy office.

Sometimes when you practice with the phrases suggested in these meditations, it can feel quite genuine; at other times, it can feel like you are merely going through the motions; at still others, phrases can bring up feelings opposite to those of the intention. You may say, "May my ex-girlfriend be happy," and what becomes clear is how much anger you are still carrying toward her. There is a clarifying aspect in practicing with these kinds of phrases, especially when they bring up uncomfortable feelings. There is also a transformative dimension as you continue to invite a shift of feelings in your heart and mind. I have found in working with many students and clients that these practices are most effective when they are specifically relevant to your personal challenges. For example, if you have just lost a loved one, these phrases are most healing when they speak with gentle caring to your personal feelings of grief.

Practicing diligently allows compassion to become an integral part of your fabric of being and, therefore, your natural way of responding to life's challenges. This description of compassion by Jack Kornfield resonates deeply with me: "Compassion arises naturally as the quivering of the heart in the face of pain, ours and another's. . . . When we come to rest in the great heart of compassion, we discover a capacity to bear witness to, suffer with, and hold dear with our own vulnerable heart the sorrows and beauties of the world."[1]

For many people, the practice of self-compassion is a crucial first step. Self-compassion gives you the encouragement to become aware of what you are thinking, feeling, and sensing, and it makes it possible for you to stay with your hurt. All the practices introduced in this book will teach you to lean into the "felt sense" of your pain while holding yourself with tenderness and care. When you learn the ability to stay with the felt sense of your hurt, then the wound itself can become a portal to deep connection and caring.

Psychologist Eugene Gendlin called the felt sense "a special kind of internal bodily awareness . . . a body-sense of meaning" that the conscious mind is initially unable to articulate.[2] The felt sense not only brings you into the present moment, but it increases relaxed alertness. The moment you experience the felt sense of painful feelings is exactly when change can happen. The felt sense helps you recognize when you are afraid, hurt, angry, or ashamed, and because of that recognition, you can begin to gain insight into the meaning that experience has for you. From the depth of this understanding, you are able to extend compassion to yourself and others. When you engage in this process, something in your way of being starts to reconfigure as you gain a healthier understanding of yourself; as a result, you become increasingly free of past hurts and fears and more open to new perspectives.

In fact, compassion practices make it possible for you to view yourself clearly and honestly. Holding yourself with an attitude of warmth affords you the courage to abstain from criticizing and judging yourself when you see how unruly your mind can be. You need courage to take on the task of working with your habits of distracting yourself and avoiding what is uncomfortable. The word *courage* comes from the root *cor*, Latin for "heart." You need a strong heart, supported by compassion and self-love, to lean with full awareness into the emotional depths of your experiences.

Cultivating compassion is ultimately necessary on the path of opening your heart to yourself and others. Yet often my clients and students ask questions like, "Compassion sounds like a great idea, but how can we get there, practically speaking?" and, "Can you show me how to heal my wounds and make friends with myself step-by-step in tangible ways?" These questions inspired me to refine and write down the following practices.

Chapter 7 presents mindfulness as formal meditation and Loving Awareness Meditation as a variation on this practice. The Loving Awareness Meditation teaches you to hold yourself with affection and warmth during the more challenging stages of Mindfulness Meditation.

Chapter 8 introduces the Mindful Pause Practice, which teaches you how to stop for a moment so you can infuse mindfulness and compassion into your daily life, especially when something has thrown you out of balance. With Mindfulness Meditation, Loving Awareness Meditation, and the Mindful Pause Practice, you set the foundation for being able to look at yourself and the world around you with clear and compassionate eyes.

Chapter 9 explains the Heart's Intention Practice. Whatever practice you engage in is made much more powerful when you undertake it with a clear intention and a meaningful purpose. With the help of the Heart's Intention Practice, you can find your way out of confusion and discover your center again.

Chapter 10 presents the Self-Compassion Practice. Your ability to be mindful and hold yourself with affectionate attention allows you to treat yourself tenderly. When you offer yourself compassion in ways that are relevant to your particular situation, you will feel more whole and strong enough to engage with your world.

Chapter 11 introduces the Compassion for Others Practice. Your compassion for others is strengthened by your courage to honor your own pain. This practice will enhance your heart's ability to care and widens the spiral of those you include in your concern. Such practice will lead not only to others' happiness but also to your own.

Chapter 12 describes the Heart That Cares for All, or Bodhichitta, Practice. This practice, based in the understanding that we are all connected to one another, assists you in further expanding and strengthening your intention. Now your insight into interdependence can become the foundation for your compassion and your desire to wake up will be for the benefit of others. Following the spirit of bodhichitta, you include the well-being of all life in your intention.

Chapter 13 presents the Compassionate Choice Practice. This practice includes a chart that helps you recognize, step-by-step, when you have been triggered. Now you can slow yourself down and bring awareness to your reactions. After taking a mindful time-out, you are able to reflect on yourself with self-compassion, hold a wider perspective, and make wiser choices. This practice helps you work with long-standing, recurrent, painful patterns—those that create havoc in your life over and over.

Chapter 14 explains the Spiral of Compassion and Forgiveness Practice. The Heart's Intention and Heart That Cares for All practices give you the fuel and direction to extend well-wishing, caring, and forgiveness to yourself and others. In the Spiral of Compassion and

Forgiveness Practice, you deepen the quality of your caring. You are able to let go of old misgivings; this frees you to love and give.

Chapter 15 provides a variety of Mindfulness On-the-Go practices. These brief practices allow you to bring mindfulness and compassion to everyday life challenges, even when you have only a few minutes to spare. The diversity of the situations presented, such as feelings of loneliness, isolation, and sadness, will allow you to see the potential for bringing mindfulness and compassion to any challenge you may face.

Each practice chapter is followed by a review of the key points and a box with a sample practice. A few journal prompts give you another opportunity to integrate the practices into your own life.

Extensive research in contemporary neuroscience demonstrates the power of repeated practice to transform the brain and the heart. Studies on mirror neurons suggest that neurons in your brain help you to experience empathy and also that your attitude toward and habits of expressing empathy can modify the neurons in your brain. Moreover, according to some researchers, neurons in your heart may have an even stronger influence on your ability to be compassionate than those in your brain. Forty thousand sensory neurons relay information from the heart to the brain. Researchers in the field of neurocardiology call the heart the "little brain."

It is important to cultivate the sensitivity of the heart through compassion practices. The neurons within the heart enable it to learn, remember, and make decisions in conjunction with, as well as independent of, the brain's cerebral cortex. *Heart* is understood here both as a neurological organ that can be transformed and as a metaphor for compassion and caring.

The research suggests that heart-focused meditations and practices can enhance your ability to care. By "educating" your heart with compassion practices, you can expand your ability to respond with natural kindness and care, regardless of the circumstances. The following nine practices will teach you in different yet complementary ways how to bring compassion into all aspects of your life.

7

Mindfulness Meditation

Mindfulness is the foundation for all other practices described in this book. Jon Kabat-Zinn, who brought mindfulness meditation into the mainstream, defines *mindfulness* as "moment-to-moment, nonjudgmental awareness."[3] This was the meditation the Buddha loved and taught most.

Mindfulness Meditation helps you to cultivate heightened awareness, tranquility, and inner happiness. You begin this practice by turning your gaze around and looking inward. Besides witnessing the always changing sensations in your body, you notice the quality of your mind, whether you are restless, alert, or drawing a blank. You notice whether you are ruminating or your mind is calm and quiet. You notice when emotions, such as sadness, anger, fear, or happiness, pass by. With mindfulness, you become kindly and patiently aware of your relationship to life. I often understand mindfulness as "affectionate attention," meaning that you learn to be present with an underlying attitude of kindness and warmth.

Steady attention to physical sensations, especially your breath, is the gateway to the present moment, the magical place where you are free from the troubles of the past and worries about the future. To come to this precious place of "now," Buddhist teacher Pema Chödrön suggests, "This is not watching the breath like a hawk; this is not about concentrating on the breath. This is feeling the breath, or any word you can use to be one with your breath."[4] What is important here is to be with the felt sense of the breath and to let yourself flow with and surrender to its sensation and movement.

As it is easier to rest in the exquisite experience of the present moment when you are relaxed rather than tense, it is helpful to attend to your out-breath. Exhaling impacts your nervous system in a way that reduces stress. Here is how Buddhist scholar and teacher Alan Wallace describes attending to the out-breath: "Let go all the way through the exhale, even beyond the end of the exhale . . . until the next breath flows in effortlessly, like a wave washing up on shore."[5]

When you align your attention with your exhalation and abdicate volition—meaning when you try neither to control nor to change the breath—then you can feel that your body breathes all by itself. As your body "breathes you," you begin to experience the interconnected and always changing nature of life. Sufi poet Kabir puts it like this: "Something inside me has reached the place where the world is breathing."[6]

With Mindfulness Meditation, you learn about the constantly changing nature of existence by noticing the constantly changing nature of your own experiences. You also learn that you can be with whatever is happening without grasping on to certain experiences or pushing away others. Ongoing Mindfulness Meditation helps you to develop a background field that is calm and kind and from which the present moments of your life emerge. As you begin to live in an aware and connected way, your skillful engagement with life will follow naturally.

HENRY'S STORY

When I first saw Henry in psychotherapy, he was going through an especially hard time in his life. The lanky, curly haired twenty-five-year-old was working as a graduate student in chemistry at our local university. Henry suffered from anxiety, depression, and insecurity. He had difficulty falling asleep, as well as staying asleep, and told me about his many worries. In addition, he was haunted by criticism from his gruff and authoritarian father. An undercurrent of anxiety and paranoia left Henry feeling uncomfortable most of the time.

When I recommended to Henry that Mindfulness Meditation might help him work with his anxiety and learn to feel more comfortable with himself, he was surprisingly open to the suggestion. During the next five years, mindfulness became a steady and ongoing practice for Henry. Being a researcher, he liked the clear, almost scientific methodology of this practice as well as the abundance of research available about its potentially positive effects on his health.

First I introduced Henry to what meditation is about. "Unlike psychotherapy, where you attend to the content of your thoughts and feelings, here you are asked to merely notice the process of your experiences," I said. "As you attend to the felt sense of your breath, you may notice that you get distracted every few seconds. You may hear noises; you may feel discomfort somewhere in your body. Thoughts, feelings, images, worries, or opinions might intrude into your consciousness."

Henry asked, "What can I do about my thoughts that keep churning around and around?"

"You learn to notice, 'thinking,' 'feeling,' 'sensing,' 'being bored,' or 'being irritated,'" I explained. "I recommend that you notice the arising, abiding, and fading away of the phenomena in your mind, as if they were leaves floating downstream on a river." Then I added, "And you learn to hold yourself with kindness, no matter how distracted your mind might be."

As is the case with most people I work with, it helped Henry to set aside a daily time for meditation practice. In doing this, he gave himself a message that his own healing and peace of mind were important. He preferred meditating in the early evening after he came home from the laboratory. Yet at times, especially after waking up from a disturbing nightmare, it was helpful for him to sweep out the cobwebs of the night with mindful breathing. He jokingly called this process "mental flossing."

In the beginning months of his practice, meditation often meant being bored, feeling pain, or falling asleep. Every few moments, his attention was hijacked by yet another sticky thought. Then he experienced a breakthrough in his practice when he truly found his breath. Henry learned to reach beyond his swirling thoughts and uncomfortable feelings for a few moments at a time by focusing his attention on the sensation of breath. Sensation does not exist in the past or in the future, but in the immediacy of the here and now.

As he began to bring his attention to sensation, Henry arrived in the present moment. This shift allowed him to experience a feeling of refuge, a moment of freedom from his tortured mind. As he allowed his awareness to be carried by the sensation of breath, his awareness became one with the breath.

With the feeling of being breathed, Henry was able to experience himself as part of a bigger, fluid, and always changing field of experience. He felt a sense of relief in noticing the fleeting nature of his thoughts, emotions, and sensations. Experiencing impermanence in this way helped him to release the tight hold he had on himself, and by not holding on to everything so tightly, he saw that there was a bigger perspective beyond the trap of his manifold small worries. It was as if the little swirl of his individual experience was now part of a bigger stream.

Key Points

- The ongoing practice of Mindfulness Meditation helps you to prepare a background field of mindful awareness.
- Sensation brings you to the present.
- Turning your gaze inward allows you to see yourself clearly.
- The breath as the primary object of awareness allows you to focus, relax, and experience yourself as part of a greater flow.
- Noticing thoughts, feelings, and images as well as other sensations allows you to see those phenomena clearly and to experience their impermanent or ever-changing nature.
- Focusing on the out-breath allows you to relax deeply.
- Mindfulness Meditation reduces stress and allows you to become more present and aware in a relaxed and alert way.
- The on-the-go Mindfulness Meditation can be practiced throughout the day.

- A formal Mindfulness Meditation practice makes it easier to practice mindful awareness on the go.
- Practicing Mindfulness Meditation on the go nourishes your commitment to formal mindfulness awareness practice.

⟶ MINDFULNESS MEDITATION

- I find a quiet and comfortable place.
- I sit in a chair, on a cushion, or on a bench, or I lie on my back on the ground.
- I keep my back straight yet allow my body to relax.
- I allow myself to settle into the sensations of my body.
- I notice my body's weight and the sensations of touch between body and chair, cushion, mat, or floor.
- I notice the sensations in my body, starting with the soles of my feet and moving upward into my legs and thighs, buttocks, back, and the front of my body.
- I let my attention move to my shoulders and let them drop with an out-breath.
- Then I move to my jaw and let it drop with an out-breath as well.
- I allow the muscles of my face to relax and my eyes to soften, and the space between my eyebrows opens up.
- I allow my whole body to be filled with a sense of being present in this moment, with spaciousness and awakeness.
- From this field of presence, I notice the natural breath arising with the inhalation, letting go with the exhalation.
- With each out-breath, I let go a little more.
- Neither changing nor controlling my breath, I notice the physical sensation of breath brushing through my body ever so gently.
- I allow my body to be breathed, allowing the breath to breathe me.
- As distractions—such as physical discomfort, thoughts, feelings, or images—arise, I notice their arising, abiding, and fading away.
- Without grasping or pushing away, I let those phenomena pass by, like clouds in the sky.

- I always return to my refuge, the breath, allowing breath to breathe me.

⤏ AN ON-THE-GO VERSION OF MINDFULNESS MEDITATION

1. I notice sensations within my body, starting with my feet.
2. I allow three natural breaths to flow through me.
3. I follow the natural sensation and movement of breath.
4. I allow my body to be breathed, allow the breath to breathe me.
5. When unpleasant thoughts or feelings carry me away, I notice this and gently return to the breath.
6. I reconnect with my body being breathed, allowing the warm breath to breathe me.
7. When I am ready, I reengage with life.

LOVING AWARENESS MEDITATION

Loving Awareness Meditation is a variation on Mindfulness Meditation in which you use the distractions of your mind as cues to extend a kind and compassionate attitude toward yourself. You extend this feeling of warmth by learning to associate emotional warmth with the felt sense of exhaling. When you find your attention wandering, take each distraction as a reminder to offer warmth and, yes, love to yourself.

Becoming highly aware of your inner experience during Mindfulness Meditation can at first seem boring, frustrating, or even overwhelming. Sometimes it may seem as if your mind is relentlessly spewing out all kinds of thoughts, feelings, and images. If you tend to be self-critical, an unskillful use of mindfulness can lead you to have a harsh attitude toward yourself, criticizing your "failure" to control your mind. Being unkind to yourself causes you to contract inside, which then undermines your ability to grow and be open to new learning. Therefore it is important to learn to cultivate a gentle, kind, or loving attitude toward yourself and toward your own process through what I call Loving Awareness Meditation.

Henry's Experience with Loving Awareness Meditation

Because Henry had suffered much harshness and criticism from his father, he tended to disapprove of himself and feel wronged by others. When his relationship with his boss, a renowned professor of mechanical engineering, became tense, Henry would lie awake at night, ruminating for hours about the possible mistakes he might have made.

Similarly, when Henry's mind became distracted during meditation, he tended to become extraordinarily impatient with himself. At those times, he regarded himself as an inefficient meditator and felt discouraged about his practice. I assured Henry that his mind's distractibility was not his fault, as we can't help how active our minds tend to be. During one session, I taught him how to do an on-the-go version of Loving Awareness Meditation.

During a guided meditation, which Henry recorded on his iPhone, I elucidated, "With each out-breath, allow yourself to experience the felt sense of compassion, of warmth for yourself. When your out-breath and the feeling of caring are paired, then they begin to flow together naturally over time.

"Your mind might meander," I said, as he closed his eyes and practiced. "There might be thoughts, emotions, images, worries, comments, or fantasies. Remember that each time your mind wanders, there is an opportunity to offer kindness and compassion to yourself. Feel the warm breath of compassion touch the area of your heart and move through the entire space of your body." I watched as Henry's face began to look relaxed and peaceful.

After working with this meditation for a while, Henry reported that the Loving Awareness Meditation had indeed helped him to develop a different attitude toward himself. For example, he was increasingly free of bouts of self-blame over his dealings with his boss. Pairing distraction with empathy had dissipated the harshness Henry felt toward himself.

With the help of Loving Awareness Meditation, Henry began to make friends with himself.

Key Points

- The Loving Awareness Meditation allows you to infuse Mindfulness Meditation with loving awareness.
- Distraction becomes your prompt to offer warmth and a sense of caring to yourself.
- The Loving Awareness Meditation allows you to use Mindfulness Meditation as a process of self-healing, which helps you to make friends with yourself.
- The on-the-go version of the Loving Awareness Meditation will allow you to use this practice when you have only brief moments of time.

◦ LOVING AWARENESS MEDITATION

- I notice the gentle breath in the area of my heart, breath breathing through like wind gently brushing through the leaves of a tree.
- With each movement of breath, I allow myself to feel a sensation and an attitude of warmth and kindheartedness for myself.
- I notice my breath expanding with the in-breath, letting go with the out-breath, the breath breathing me with warmth and a sense of caring for myself.
- I notice my mind wandering—thoughts, feelings, images, and daydreams arising.
- Whenever I notice any of these distractions with kind, nonjudgmental awareness, I allow myself to be present to what is. I relax and remember the sensation of breath, of warmth and caring for myself, brushing through my heart.
- When I am fully focused on the sensation of breath, I allow my whole body to be breathed, letting the sensation move me ever so gently.

- I continue to breathe, returning to the relaxed, caring breath, filled with warmth around the area of my heart, whenever my mind wanders and becomes distracted. I hold myself lightly and with a sense of friendship.
- I meditate like this for a while.

⟿ AN ON-THE-GO VERSION OF THE LOVING AWARENESS MEDITATION

1. I notice sensations within my body.
2. I allow three natural breaths to flow through me.
3. I feel the gentle sensation of the out-breath brush through my heart.
4. With each out-breath, I connect to a sense of warmth and caring.
5. When unpleasant thoughts or feelings carry me away, I remember the sensation of loving awareness.
6. I connect with my body being breathed and allow the warm breath to breathe through me.
7. When I am ready, I reengage with life.

JOURNAL EXERCISE

Sit down with a pencil and paper in a quiet place. Make yourself comfortable, rest in your gentle breath, and see what images and stories arise as you read the following prompts. If your own experiences come to mind, do some free writing.

1. Describe your experiences with Mindfulness Meditation.
2. Write about some of the obstacles you have encountered.
3. When thoughts come up and you allow them to pass by while trying not to grasp them, notice what happens.
4. After practicing the Loving Awareness Meditation, describe your experience.

8

The Mindful Pause Practice

The mindful pause is another foundational practice; it is fundamental to all other practices that will follow in this book. This practice has a twofold purpose. First, a mindful pause interrupts a reactive moment while helping you find your balance again. Second, as brief, intermittent, intentional intermissions during your day, mindful pauses help you to raise the flow of your awareness during the course of daily events.

Let's first talk about when the mindful pause helps you in upsetting moments to suspend your reactivity and regain your balance. This practice is a way to bring mindfulness, compassion, and a relaxed calmness to the present moment when you need it most. This can allow you to find a renewed sense of steadiness even in stressful moments.

When you are triggered and your own impulsivity surprises you in the midst of a busy day, you probably don't have the luxury to take time out and sit in meditation for an hour or even twenty minutes at a time. You may only have a few moments to calm and center yourself. A mindful pause can take any kind of shape or form. The important aspect is that this intentional break can help you break in on the reactive feelings you are experiencing, such as incessant circular thinking or strong feelings of anger, fear, rage, or frustration.

Choosing to practice the mindful pause can allow you to bring compassionate awareness to your internal state on more occasions during your waking hours. By taking a break and sharpening your awareness, you can rebalance yourself. This makes it possible for you to reengage in life with wisdom and compassion.

The most effective way to interrupt your reactive feelings is to refocus yourself on the present moment. The sequence of noticing your body, breath, and feelings and extending compassion to yourself helps to bring structure and presence to the pause. By following the sequence, you become aware of when it is the right time to reengage with life. As you become familiar with this sequence and it becomes a new habit for you, taking a mindful pause can increasingly become your automatic way of responding.

This way of transforming reactivity is supported by an ongoing meditation practice and by the other purpose of the Mindful Pause Practice, which is introducing brief, intentional breaks in the flow of your day by giving you moments of opportunity to help yourself wake up and bring mindfulness to your present experience.

There are many different ways you can choose to press the pause button intermittently during your day. For regular people in a busy world, there is usually only time for a brief intermission. Such a pause could consist of deliberately walking down the corridor to the bathroom, washing your hands attentively, carefully taking out the paper towel, or walking to the lunchroom mindfully. During those fleeting moments, you might use a few short phrases, such as the following:

• Noticing my body, feeling my heart and compassion for self

or

• Exhaling to relax, gentling the heart, finding time to balance.

Applying mindfulness to regular, recurring activities in your life can help bring awareness to times of stress. Every time before she sends an e-mail, one of my friends says quietly to herself,

- Noticing my body, breathing through my heart, living peace.

She reports that this ritual helps her to be more mindful of what she writes in her e-mails.

My husband has set up his phone so that several times a day it rings with the phrase,

- May all beings be happy.

He says that this ritual helps him with his work as a palliative care doctor.

The Vietnamese Zen master Thich Nhat Hahn recommends using little poems, also called *gathas*, to support experiencing many mindful pauses throughout the day. You could say a phrase quietly to yourself, such as *Present moment, wonderful moment.* Thich Nhat Hahn recommends the following phrases when you are sitting in your car before turning it on or when you take out your recycling:[7]

⌖ BEFORE STARTING THE CAR

- I know where I am going.
- The car and I are one.
- If the car goes fast, I go fast.

⌖ RECYCLING

- In the garbage, I see the rose.
- In the rose I see the garbage.
- Everything is transformation.
- Even permanence is impermanent.

Feel free to become creative and develop relevant and accessible phrases that support you in bringing awareness to your regular activities. The more presence you bring to routine events through Mindful Pause

Practice, the easier it will be to stay conscious during times when you are triggered.

ED'S STORY

Several months ago, when my thirty-seven-year-old client Ed attended a seminar in which I taught the Mindful Pause Practice, he told me the following story. He had unexpectedly run into his ex-girlfriend in the grocery store. Ed and Leyla had separated one year earlier under painful circumstances. Ed had felt betrayed and disrespected by Leyla. Therefore, when faced with a surprise run-in with her, he was thrown completely out of balance.

That day, when Ed discovered that Leyla was standing behind a mountain of green and red apples in the grocery store, he tried to avoid her. But each time he turned a corner to get something he needed in the store, she was standing there ready to engage him.

When Ed left the store, he felt terrible. His heart was pounding, his chest felt contracted, and his mind was racing.

That same evening, he was invited to a dear friend's family dinner. He had not seen this friend in a long time and dreaded going to dinner in the state he was in. During the twenty-minute drive to his friend's house, Ed noticed how much he was feeling out of sorts. He felt a weight on his chest, and his hands were trembling. Recognizing that he had been seriously triggered, he made the decision to pause. He pulled his car over and read the laminated Brief Mindful Pause sticker on his dashboard.

⌒ WHEN I FEEL TRIGGERED

1. I notice my body.
2. I choose to pause.
3. I exhale gently to relax.
4. I recognize my feelings.
5. I sense my heart.

6. I offer compassion to myself.
7. When I am ready, I reengage.

For a moment, Ed just sat in his car. He felt his body touching the seat and the subtle movements of his breath. He noticed the sensation of his out-breath touching his internal organs ever so lightly. With each exhalation, he sank more deeply into himself. His tension started to dissipate.

Then Ed became aware of the tightness and heaviness in his chest. Gradually he felt breath brushing through his lungs. He noticed that his heart felt tight and constricted like an iron fist. He realized how frustrated he was and how much hurt remained deep inside. With each out-breath, he started to feel a sense of warmth. A sense of tenderness replaced the self-loathing and frustration. *Exhale, compassion*, he said silently. *I sense warmth breathing through like wind brushing through the leaves of a tree.*

Something in Ed let go, and he was able to relax a bit. He continued to sit for a few more minutes, quietly enjoying the motion of being breathed. He started to feel better and began to look forward to seeing his friend. Ed started the car and drove on.

Key Points

- You learn to recognize that you have been triggered.
- By attending to the felt sense of your body, you ground yourself in the present moment.
- Know that you can make the choice to pause instead of react.
- The out-breath allows you to relax.
- When you lean into the felt sense of your emotions, you are in the present moment where transformation can occur.
- Compassion for yourself helps you to make friends with yourself.
- Only you know when you are ready to reengage.

∽ THE MINDFUL PAUSE PRACTICE

When I Feel Triggered

1. I notice my body.
2. I choose to pause.
3. I exhale gently to relax.
4. I recognize my feelings.
5. I sense my heart.
6. I offer compassion to myself.
7. When I am ready, I reengage.

JOURNAL EXERCISE

Sit down with a pencil and paper in a quiet place. Make yourself comfortable, rest in your gentle breath, and see what images and stories arise as you read the following prompts. If your own experiences come to mind, do some free writing.

1. Describe an event when you were reactive and wished you had not been.
2. Take a few deep and gentle breaths. Now imagine what it would be like if you, in the situation you just described, had excused yourself for a few minutes and found a quiet place to engage in Mindful Pause Practice. How might the event have played out differently?
3. Imagine integrating an ongoing meditation practice and the use of the mindful pause into your life. Describe one or more situations that you might navigate in a different way.

The Heart's Intention Practice

The Heart's Intention Practice will help you direct your life in the ways that matter most to you. This practice is especially useful when you feel self-doubt or fear or when you are confused about which path to choose. In such circumstances, your mind and heart may feel clouded, your mind distracted by obsessive ruminations and your heart torn by strong emotions.

Let's first understand the role of intention. You set your intentions based on your deepest values and make a commitment to align what you do in the world with what matters deeply to you. When I first came to America, I did not know which career path to pursue, whether I wanted to go back into practicing medicine or train to become a midwife, an acupuncturist, or a psychotherapist. I knew that I wanted to help heal others' suffering, just as I had received healing. My heart's intention was therefore to be in a profession in which I could follow this calling. As I contemplated my intention, I gradually discerned what my gifts were and how I could best serve in a way that was enjoyable and fulfilling to me. During this time of self-discernment, I realized that I was interested in bridging psychological and spiritual ways of understanding and healing human suffering.

There is a difference between intentions and goals. While intentions are rooted in the understanding of what you find meaningful as your deep inner values, goals are directed toward future outcomes and help you to organize your life to become a productive member of society. Goals can pull you toward what is outside yourself, while your intentions anchor you inside. If you remember to return again and again to the depth of your intentions, your goals will become wiser, and you will find a sense of integrity and meaning in your life. Then your goals will support your intentions and follow their creative lead.

Getting a doctorate in clinical psychology, applying myself in internships that trained me as a clinician, and getting a California license were goals that supported my heart's intention to heal suffering. Yet I realized that to fulfill my deeper intention to contribute to the relief of others' suffering, I needed to bridge Buddhist and Western psychology. After I practiced as psychologist for a while, I realized that I wanted to study dharma and meditation practice more deeply so I could eventually guide others. I found a mentor and investigated my inner life during long retreats and profound psychotherapy.

Gradually I realized that I wanted to contribute to making mindfulness accessible to busy people leading ordinary lives. Studying with Alan Wallace and Paul Ekman, I explored how thoughts and emotions work and how to cultivate emotional balance. Guided by my heart's intention to be able to help my clients and students with their daily challenges, both my professional and spiritual roads gained momentum, and my goals became increasingly well defined.

As I have forged my own life, I have continued to explore the relationship between intentions and goals. Intentions lead you to create goals for yourself, and goals in turn support your intentions.

An old Chinese proverb describes the importance of intentions and how they determine the direction your life takes: "Intentions bring about behaviors, behaviors lead to habits, habits form personality, and your personality shapes your destiny, which is the way your life unfolds." Forming intentions is like planting seeds. Your goals help organize the behaviors and the actions you take, allowing the seeds to grow into big trees.

LARRY'S STORY

Larry, a psychotherapy and meditation client, looked at me with a pained and confused expression on his face. "I need to figure out whether I can be open about being gay. My daughters are coming this August," he explained.

I told Larry that I thought the Heart's Intention Practice would help him in this tricky situation.

Ten years earlier, Larry had moved from a small town in the Midwest to San Francisco. The years during which he had been hiding his sexual orientation from his military father, from the church in which he had been brought up, and from most of the people in his small town had been agonizing. Being married had given him some protection, yet the stress of living a false life had become too difficult to bear.

Eventually he left the marriage and two little daughters, Mary and Kristie, to move to San Francisco, where he could live openly as a gay man. A few years later, he and his boyfriend, Stefano, had moved to Santa Barbara. Being in California, he enjoyed his newfound freedom and ability to live authentically, yet he missed his little daughters very much. Every summer they would visit their dad. Before they arrived, Larry would "sanitize" his apartment, hiding gay literature, photos with friends, and artwork, and he would ask Stefano to move out for a month. This ordeal of changing his identity for his daughters had become more and more upsetting for Larry over the years, especially as Stefano did not want to be sent away for a full month year after year.

Sitting in my big brown chair, Larry was confused and in disarray. "What should I do?" he asked. "I don't want to lose Stefano over this, and I don't want to lose my daughters."

I responded, "I understand that you are upset and that loss has been a painful theme in your life. Yet maybe there is a chance for a positive outcome if you tell your daughters about your sexual orientation." Then I added, "Your girls are now fourteen and sixteen years old, and I bet may already know their father is gay."

"Oh, I don't think so," Larry blurted out. "They come from a very small town in the Bible Belt, and their mother has involved them in her conservative church." He sighed. "I feel so beside myself, not knowing how to handle this situation."

Later during the session, Larry was flooded with memories of times when, due to his colorful and feminine style as a teenager, his mother had withheld her love and his dad had chastised him. At that point, Larry went underground, being extra careful to hide anything that could reveal his true inclinations. He got married early and for many years lived a false and concealed existence. Eight years later, after a serious car accident, he woke up and realized what he was doing. Sick and depressed, Larry decided to move to San Francisco. His family chose not to tell the girls about their father's true way of life. He still felt the grief and shame of that decision.

Toward the end of the session, I asked Larry about his meditation practice, as I knew that meditating would be an important support during this difficult time. He had started meditating a few years earlier, and both he and Stefano had participated in "cultivating emotional balance" training the previous year. I told Larry that I regarded a daily practice as the foundation for finding his balance and a sense of inner calm, as well as a way to root himself in a much wider perspective.

But Larry needed more support than the suggestion to return to his daily meditation. He asked, "How can I find my way forward in the midst of these difficult and confusing feelings? I feel that I need a direction to go forward."

I asked him if he was willing to work with the Heart's Intention Practice as a way of discerning wise steps forward in a healthy direction for his old and new families. I explained the difference between intentions and goals and said that it might be helpful if he could learn to ground himself in his heart's intentions. Then I offered to guide him through the Heart's Intention Practice. After he relaxed in his chair and began to sense his body and breath, I led him through the following practice:

─◦ THE HEART'S INTENTION PRACTICE

When I Feel Confused

- I sense my body.
- I recognize with kindness the passing of thoughts and feelings of fear, self-doubt, and confusion.
- I calm my heart with the gentleness of my out-breath.
- I feel my own suffering and offer compassion to myself.
- I allow breath to move through my body ever so gently, connecting me to the bigger flow of life.
- I recognize my deepest yearning for being in balance with myself; close with my girls; and in loving harmony with my new family, Stefano.
- I sense my longing to align my life—with true meaning and purpose—with my heart's intention.
- I feel the breath of my heart.
- Deep inside, I know what would assist me to feel in balance again.
- I allow breath to move through my body; I allow life to breathe me.

After this meditation, Larry was quiet for a while. When he opened his eyes, he said, "This was very interesting. Sensing my own pain, even despair, helped a lot. My anxiety calmed down as I offered myself understanding and empathy. I realized how heavy the burden of shame and loneliness has been, and I've been carrying it for so long." For a moment Larry sat there quietly. "I know now that I want to live a life with integrity, without lies and with love." After a short while he added, "Can you help me do that?"

Larry realized that his heart's intention was to live an authentic life in which he could express his love to all the people he cared about so deeply. He did not want to live a lie anymore. His goals were to find practical and effective ways to show his girls who he really was while communicating to Stefano how much he wanted Stefano to be part of his life. Together we made a plan to have one or more family sessions during the time his girls were visiting. The goal was that I would help Larry to tell his girls the truth about his sexual orientation.

The outcome was surprising to him. Making an internal shift in relation to his heart's intention must have loosened some pent-up tension and released trapped energy. During the family session, he was able to be clear and very kind.

The girls said that they had figured out some years earlier that their father was gay. They laughed and felt relieved that the lies and secrets were over. Larry's oldest daughter said, "Do you think we are living on the moon? We are modern women."

Together they redecorated Larry's apartment, and Stefano came for dinner. Two weeks later, while the girls were still there, Stefano moved back in. As the awkwardness was gone and they felt much more comfortable, the girls decided they did not want to wait a year to visit again. They decided to come for Christmas vacation.

Key Points

- The Heart's Intention Practice allows you to discern your intentions, the deep values of your heart.
- These intentions will give power and direction to your spiritual practice as well as to your life.
- Your heart's intentions will inspire you to make practical, step-by-step goals.
- These goals will in turn support your heart's intention.
- Wise intentions arise from an ongoing practice that is clear and filled with mindfulness and compassion.

∽ THE HEART'S INTENTION PRACTICE

When I Feel Full of Doubt and Bewildered

- I notice the sensations of distress in my body.
- I exhale gently to relax.

- I recognize my feelings of confusion and doubt with kind awareness.
- I linger with the felt sense of confusion and suffering.
- I pause to offer compassion to myself and hold my confusion with patience and kindness.
- I feel the breath of my heart lightly flowing through me.
- I am able to feel what is deeply meaningful to me.
- I am able to discern my heart's intention.
- I connect with breath as a refuge.
- When I am ready, I reengage with life.

JOURNAL EXERCISE

Sit down with a pencil and paper in a quiet place. Make yourself comfortable, rest in your gentle breath, and see what images and stories arise as you read the following prompts. If your own experiences come to mind, do some free writing.

1. Think about an area of your life that feels unclear and confusing to you. Write a few sentences about your feelings of doubt and confusion. Then finish this sentence: "What I really long for is . . ." This will help you go beneath thoughts to a deeper level of discernment.

2. Use the Heart's Intention Practice in the box above and write about your dilemma by following the steps of the practice. Be sure to stay connected and aware of the feelings in your body, and see how your feelings change as you work through your dilemma.

The Self-Compassion Practice

In the meditation on self-compassion, you learn to cultivate a sense of tenderness for your own suffering, which is an essential step in including others and the world in your care. With the help of carefully guided meditations, you will discover how to offer a deep sense of understanding and warmth to yourself in ways that are relevant to your particular challenges.

The Buddha called *compassion* "tenderness of heart." With compassion, your heart and mind can gradually soften. You will begin a process of healing by first offering the quality of tenderness to yourself. Once you have learned how to make friends with yourself, you are better able to widen your compassion to others.

Psychologist John Welwood wrote, "You can't have compassion unless you're first willing to feel what you feel."[8] When you allow even your uncomfortable and messy emotions into your awareness, you become open and vulnerable in a gentle way. It can be helpful to be truly humbled by the reality of your feelings. By leaning into the felt sense of your emotions, you enter the present moment. When you are truly present with yourself, transformation can happen.

Allowing yourself to become aware of the feeling tone of what is difficult gives you the opportunity to become grounded in the humanity all of us share. Rather than difficult or messy emotions being problems, they are the grist for the mill of your inner work. Within that so-called messiness, you have the opportunity to become truly compassionate toward yourself, others, and the world.

Often you may not be aware that you have succumbed to the habit of self-criticism. Your parents and grandparents may have had a harsh pattern of relating, and you may be equally accustomed to harshness when it comes to speaking to yourself. Also, you may have been told that self-criticism is a way to control yourself. You may be afraid that you will become reckless and irresponsible without the whip of self-deprecation.

However, self-chastisement is not a good tool for keeping yourself in check. Having a critical attitude toward yourself can make you frustrated, depressed, anxious, guilty, and ashamed. When you criticize, undercut, or condemn yourself, much of your vitality—which you urgently need to heal and engage with the world—is thwarted.

When you practice self-compassion, you are willing to be present with all that you are, in your body, in this moment, no matter how uncomfortable it may be. Instead of fighting life (and yourself), you learn to notice it and allow it to pass through in its own time. Being gentle with yourself allows you to witness what is happening with caring eyes rather than habitually contracting from judgment or reacting out of fear. Now your energy has a chance to replenish.

The Loving-Kindness and Self-Compassion practices described in this chapter can be seen as two sides of the same coin. With Loving-Kindness Practice, you wish yourself (and then others) well, whereas with the Self-Compassion Practice, you feel your (and then another's) suffering. His Holiness the Dalai Lama tells us, "Compassion and love can be defined as the positive thoughts and feelings that give rise to such essential things in life as hope, courage, determination and inner strength. Compassion is the wish for another being to be free from suffering, love is wanting others to have happiness."[9]

I sometimes imagine the Loving-Kindness and Self-Compassion practices as two arms that hold you. One arm supports you from below, while the other arm protects and blesses you from above. Loving-kindness says,

- May you be well.

Compassion says,

- May I offer you caring when you are in pain.

You need both to heal.

CARMEN'S STORY

Carmen, a woman in her early fifties with curly brown hair and a warm voice, had received the diagnosis of advanced breast cancer a year before she came to see me. Even though she had been a dedicated meditation practitioner for a long time, she now had a hard time bringing the meditative skills to the challenges of surgery and chemotherapy. Lymphedema had caused pain in her right arm, and the aftereffects of chemotherapy had left her feeling drained and tired. With her shoulders hunched and a faint sigh, she told me in our first session that she had been feeling increasingly down and depleted.

When I asked Carmen if she could tell me about her relationship toward herself, she started to cry. "Often I just want to run from the discomfort in my arm, the feeling of exhaustion, and the always present anxiety," she admitted quietly. "It is so important for me to stay connected to myself and my daughter, yet sometimes I just can't."

Feeling shut off from her sixteen-year-old daughter was unbearable to Carmen, because as a single mom, she felt especially close to Angelica. However, when she became scared, she would retreat to a contracted place inside herself.

Carmen talked about the sense of betrayal she felt toward herself and life and how difficult that was. "I was left feeling lost, without a purpose," she said. "That was the deepest kind of loneliness I ever experienced—to be alienated from myself and from life itself."

I asked her when she first started feeling like this.

"Well, first there was shock," she recalled. "Everything was becoming really thick, and then fear crept in. Fear of abandoning those I love. Then shame slithered in silently, which is the feeling of 'what did I do wrong to deserve this,' and a sense of being flawed."

As I knew that Carmen was open to meditation, I asked if she would allow me to guide her in a Self-Compassion Practice. I explained that this kind of meditation might help her to reconnect with herself and that compassion would be a safe container for her deep sense of vulnerability. I told her that this practice would help her to lean gently into whatever feelings she might have. I suggested that she could record the meditation on her iPhone so she could practice at home.

I first helped Carmen to relax in the big brown chair and to feel the sensations in her body. She placed her right hand on her heart and her left hand on her belly. After settling into the sensation and movement of her breath, we moved toward the practice of self-compassion meditation. Gently, I encouraged her to hold herself with an attitude of kindness and caring. I asked her to pull up an image of herself in her mind's eye and to observe kindly whatever came up. "Can you recognize what is currently challenging for you and what feelings might be there?" I asked her. Carmen exhaled a long, low breath, and I saw a tear running down her cheek.

Then I guided her in a self-compassion meditation and asked her to repeat the following phrases silently to herself after me and to notice the feelings or sensations that arose:

- May I hold myself with gentle care.
- May I hold myself with compassion, even when I feel vulnerable.
- May I extend tenderness toward myself as I experience this challenge to my body and life.

- May I be free from suffering and all its causes.
- May I continue my life with ease.

Carmen started to cry again and spontaneously rubbed the area of her heart with her right hand. I asked her to keep sensing her breath flowing through and to follow its natural movement: breath expanding with the inhalation, letting go with the exhalation, breath like a breeze brushing through the leaves of a tree.

I rang the bell and waited for Carmen to be present in the room with me again. She said that she had not felt connected to herself in this way for a long while and how grateful she was. She added that it was hard for her to experience so much vulnerability but that allowing herself to feel it now was comforting. We decided that this was enough work for one day, and we would meet in the coming week. Carmen took her recording and left.

When she returned to my office later that week, she told me that she liked the phrases very much, but she found it difficult to offer love to her body. "My body right now is like an alien thing," Carmen murmured. "How can I love it?" I noticed the deep pain caused by her feeling of separation from herself. We also talked about the anger she felt toward her body for not functioning as she thought it should. She mentioned the discomfort and swelling in her right arm and her awful exhaustion. She confessed that deep inside she felt out of control. The insecurity her illness had caused Angelica, her daughter, was difficult for her to bear.

I had an idea. Even though it was not possible for Carmen to feel love toward her own body, maybe it would be possible for her to feel tenderness toward Angelica's body if she imagined Angelica hurting. I said, "I see that it is difficult to bring tenderness to your own body. How would it be if Angelica's young body were wounded in some way? Was there a time when that happened?"

After a brief silence, Carmen answered, "Yes, there was a time six years ago, when Angelica had a ruptured appendix. Her tummy was inflamed; she had a high fever, great pain, and was in the hospital for more than a week."

I said, "Can you imagine Angelica in a big hospital bed, in pain, with fever, scared for you to leave? See what it is like to offer compassion to her suffering body."

- May you, Angelica, be safe.
- May you, Angelica, be free from suffering.
- May I offer your sweet, wounded body the gentleness and care it needs to heal.

Tears poured from Carmen's eyes. She gently rubbed her heart. "I love her so much," she said. "I can send healing love imagining her fragile body."

I then asked Carmen to see whether the following offering felt right to her:

- Just as I offer Angelica's wounded body my tender care, may I also hold my own wounded body with love again.
- Just as I offer respect and love to Angelica, may I also offer respect and love to myself.
- May I hold the intention that one day I can feel affection for my body, heart, and mind again.

Carmen sat for a while in the big brown chair. She whispered, while continuing to cry, "It is so much easier to feel love and compassion for Angelica than for myself. But feeling for Angelica helped me to feel for myself." She asked if together we could formulate some phrases that would help her continue to cultivate self-compassion. These were the phrases we came up with:

- May my heart be full of love and kindness.
- May I be free from inner and outer danger to my body, heart, and mind.
- May I tend to myself during this trying time with loving care.
- May I be able to love my body as it is right now.

- May I hold the intention to love my body even as it is so wounded.
- May I embrace my fear with tender care as I am patient with my great sense of vulnerability.
- May Angelica and I live with freedom and ease.

Key Points

- Self-compassion is the movement of your heart when experiencing your own pain and sorrow.
- Cultivating self-compassion softens your heart and allows you to make friends with yourself.
- Self-compassion allows you to experience the felt sense of what you are experiencing, however painful it may be.
- When you can feel the felt sense of your pain and stay with it, something within you unlocks and your heart can open.
- The Loving-Kindness and Self-Compassion practices are two sides of the same coin. With the Loving-Kindness Practice, you wish yourself (and another) well, whereas with the Self-Compassion Practice, you feel your own (and another's) suffering.
- The dynamic of love and compassion can unfold as a widening spiral, starting with yourself and extending to others and the world.

⟶ THE LOVING-KINDNESS PRACTICE

- May my heart be full of love and kindness.
- May I live my life with ease.
- May I be free from inner and outer danger to my body, heart, and mind.
- May my mind and heart be free from sticky thoughts and feelings.
- May I accept my life with all its challenges and opportunities.
- May my mind and heart be open like the sky to all that flows through.

- May I be free from suffering and the causes of suffering.
- May I find the support I need. May life rise up to meet me.

◦ THE SELF-COMPASSION PRACTICE

- May I tend to myself during this trying time with loving care.
- May I offer compassion to myself, especially when I feel vulnerable.
- May I extend caring toward myself when I feel scared and lonely.
- May I be able to hold my fear with tender care.
- May I hold myself with gentleness and friendship.
- May I hold my sense of shame, guilt, and insecurity with gentleness and understanding.
- May I take care of my body so it will be healthy and well.
- May I give myself the gift of tending to myself.
- May I be free from suffering and the causes of suffering.
- May I receive the support I need.
- May life rise up to meet us all.

JOURNAL EXERCISE

Sit down with a pencil and paper in a quiet place. Make yourself comfortable, rest in your gentle breath, and see what images and stories arise as you read the following prompts. If your own experiences come to mind, do some free writing.

1. Describe a time when you longed for self-compassion.
2. Imagine that you offered self-compassion to yourself at that time.
3. If you were able to offer self-compassion to yourself, what happened?
4. If you found it difficult to offer yourself self-compassion, what were the obstacles that prevented you?
5. Describe what happens when you hold the intention to one day, maybe way in the future, regard yourself with gentleness and care.

The Compassion for Others Practice

As your wounded heart begins to heal with self-compassion, it may begin to fill with generosity and kindness; the boundaries of your self-preoccupation may loosen, and compassion for yourself can naturally widen to compassion for others.

The writer and psychologist Kristin Neff, who has developed impressive programs in self-compassion, writes, "Acknowledgement of the interconnected nature of our lives—indeed of life itself—helps to distinguish self-compassion from mere self-acceptance or self-love. Although self-acceptance and self-love are important, they are incomplete by themselves. They leave out an essential factor—other people."[10]

The Dalai Lama emphasizes that compassion originates in the understanding that we all are interdependent with everything that is alive. Interdependence is grounded in the concept that nothing is separate from anything else. From a Native American viewpoint, our original instruction as humans and animals is to live in interdependence and not as separate beings. That is why you may feel more complete inside when you practice compassion.

Wisdom includes insight into interdependence, and compassion is how your heart perceives and expresses interdependence. When you realize in your body and heart that you and I are not separate and that we are part of an interdependent, benevolent field, then the wish for the well-being of others and compassion for their distress arises naturally.

There are traditional Buddhist practices for developing your metaphorical heart muscle, or compassion. We all need to find our own ways into this practice. Customarily this is done by following the sequence of extending compassion to self, a loved one, a neutral person, a difficult person, and finally the world.

While for many of you it may be helpful to start with compassion for yourself and your own predicament, others may find a different doorway to compassion more accessible. Compassion for your beloved child or pet might be more readily available as a beginning step.

Compassion for yourself was discussed in the previous chapter. In the traditional sequence, the next step is to expand compassion out toward someone who is easy for you to love or someone who shares your sorrows.

From there, you may carefully widen the scope of your compassion— for example, to someone you generally like, even though you do not know her or him well. This person might be someone you have encountered briefly in a doctor's office or the supermarket.

The next step is to extend compassion to those who pose a difficulty for you. They may be groups who have attributes or attitudes that make you uncomfortable. A particular person or group you know, who holds moral views you disagree with, may feel especially unlikable to you.

The last group to extend your compassion toward is the world of sentient beings beyond those you already know, including fellow humans, other mammals, reptiles, birds, and fish. I personally regard our earth, including the trees that give us oxygen and the air that gives us life, as a sentient being as well.

In my work with clients and students, where I relate closely with a great variety of people and their very individual challenges, I include these traditional practices and also meditations and prayers designed to meet individuals' personal difficulties and sufferings. When you want to send compassion to someone who angers you or toward whom you have complicated feelings, your compassion practice needs to be tailored to the feelings you are experiencing. If you have felt hurt by a particular person, she may be the hardest to include in the caring of your heart. It can be especially challenging to send compassion to someone in your family, your circle of friends, or your work life with whom you are in conflict.

Sometimes, when extending a heartfelt feeling is too much of a stretch for you, it is helpful to start with an intention to offer compassion. A beginning step might be to set the intention that one day you will be able to offer that problematic person true compassion. You might use a phrase such as, "May I hold the intention to offer you compassion at some time to come."

It is most helpful in these individual compassion prayers to create the phrases that allow you to extend compassion in a way that is as relevant, as accessible, and as specific as possible. Then you are more likely to experience the feeling tone of those phrases in your heart. For example, when you offer compassion to a person you know who suffers from great insecurity after having lost his job, you might say as part of your morning practice,

- May you find the courage you need as you face your fear.
- May you be loved and sustained by those close to you in this time of uncertainty.
- May you experience the strength to navigate this trying situation wisely.

When you are creating phrases of compassion for a friend who is going through a divorce, you might pray,

- May you find inner stability in times of change.
- May your sorrow be met with compassion and care.
- May you and your family find a new sense of balance.

When you feel compassion for a friend's teenage child who has had brushes with the law, you might pray,

- May you be free from inner and outer danger.
- May you develop inner resources of stability and peace.
- May you find the support you need to learn and grow.

Fundamental to the practices offered in this book is the understanding that your own suffering can open you to being more compassionate toward others. Especially when you learn to hold your own suffering with gentleness and self-compassion, your own wounds can become a gateway for a deeper capacity to touch others with your caring. At some point in your life, you too may have lost your job, suffered times of separation, or had a child in trouble.

The "wounded healer" is an ancient archetype of someone whose own wounding has become the source of his or her ability to care about and for others. Tending to your own wound with kindness and insight allows you to understand and care for others who have been wounded in similar ways.

Wounded healers reenvision their own woundedness. Rather than feeling defeated, bitter, or defensive, they know their wounds can, paradoxically, become a source of strength and health, allowing tenderness of heart to be present while staying open to another's pain.

It is possible that when you are experiencing your darkest hour, you may finally soften into a gentle place within your own heart. Ironically, it is in those times that you can find something in yourself begins to open. I think of a line from Mary Oliver's poem "Dreams," "When deep in the tree all the locks click open, / and the fire surges through the wood, / and the blossoms blossom."[11] From a place of contraction inside yourself, you may be able to open up with a new feeling of sensitivity and caring.

You might consider including Joanna Macy's Breathing Through Meditation as part of your practice in opening up to painful experiences and connecting to the flow of life. Macy developed this practice to help social activists deal with witnessing overwhelming distress. It helps you to open up and let suffering flow through you; at the same time, you connect to the experience of your own little breath as part of the shared exchange that is at the heart of life on earth. It is a way of learning both to be present with great suffering and to let go so your capacity to hold witness can be nourished.

The Breathing Through Meditation allows you to let pain pass through you freely as it is carried by the breath-stream and teaches you a new kind of resilience by relating to the world in all its manifestations. By opening and surrendering to the big flow of life, you allow breath to wash through you. You release things you have been holding on to—often in painful ways—and let them flow into and become part of a much bigger context of interbeing.[12] This practice helps you realize that when you feel connected and part of something greater—even if it is simply your own breath—you can be present to the pain of others.

To be an activist, even in relation to your own life, requires being open to what is painful rather than armoring yourself against it, and without holding on to others' (or your own) suffering. The Breathing Through Meditation can be part of your care of both others and yourself. As you let go of distress to let it join the bigger stream of life with the out-breath, the resistance you may be experiencing in the face of your own or another's misery may flip into an experience of belonging and love.

LYDIA'S STORY

This is the story of a mother who desperately wanted to feel compassion for her troubled daughter. This woman had to look at her own troubled heart to discover her inner wounded healer. Only then was she able to find the sensitivity and openness to offer compassion to her daughter.

"We took Tina to the emergency room last night. Someone had found her in a parking lot, high on drugs." Lydia's face flushed with embarrassment as she spoke, then tears started to well up. Her daughter Tina has had a long struggle with heroin. Several inpatient stays had depleted the family's savings. They were emotionally and financially at their wit's end. "I don't know what to do anymore," Lydia said, as she sobbed.

When Lydia thought of her daughter, she felt overwhelmed. For some years, she had tried to do anything for Tina to help her survive. "I don't know how to keep my heart open to Tina," she confided. "I feel so frustrated and angry with her. If I could, I would like to move away and forget that she exists." Lydia released a long, jagged breath. "But I can't." She described Tina in the emergency room the night before as "so messed up and out of it." A cut on the girl's head had left her tinted blond hair encrusted with blood; her face had been bruised and smeared with mascara.

I felt the anguish of this parent and realized that, first of all, she needed my compassion as well as my nonjudgmental acceptance. "It must be difficult for you to keep your heart open. The last few years must have been devastating for you and the family."

"Yes, our family is practically destroyed," Lydia replied. "My husband is stuck in front of the TV all night, or he goes out with his buddies. My other children moved away, not wanting to have anything to do with this calamity. I feel as if nobody is really here with me."

Before Lydia could feel compassion for Tina, she first needed to acknowledge her resentment and grief. I offered Lydia the following phrases of self-compassion:

- May I be compassionate with myself as I feel anger and sorrow.
- May I, one day, live my life again with freedom and ease.

I knew how burned out Lydia felt and how hard it was for her to have authentic feelings for Tina. Lydia's heart seemed buried under layers of numbness, frustration, and repulsion. At the same time, I knew how much she wanted to feel love for her daughter again. I proposed to Lydia that it might help to begin her practice by extending the intention to feel affection and caring for Tina again one day.

"I can do that." Lydia nodded.

We agreed on the following phrases for her to use:

- May I hold the intention that one day my heart will be full of tenderness and love for Tina again.
- May I stay open and keep holding the vision that one day Tina and I will share our love again.

Lydia looked into my eyes, and said, "Deep down, even now I know I care very much. Saying those phrases made me realize that. I see Tina as the little girl she was at four years old, so sweet with her pigtails. Can we add some phrases of compassion?"

Together we formulated the following phrases:

- May you, Tina, find healing and balance in your heart.
- May you, Tina, find the support you need to be healthy and free once again.

Lydia was struggling to set clear boundaries for Tina, so she would not be enabling her daughter's drug habit. She came up with the following phrase:

- May I, Lydia, be able to offer you warmth and care, while also keeping healthy limits that are good for you and me.

I sensed that it might also help Lydia to widen her perspective. To focus only on your own predicament can make you feel lonely and separate. To include others allows you to see yourself within a wider, interconnected view. I asked her to think of mothers, fathers, and grandparents in similar predicaments and to extend compassion toward them. Lydia told me about the other parents she had met in various rehabilitation centers and how their stories had been so very sad, like hers. I guided her in the following meditation, while encouraging her to expand her compassion to the many others who are living with similar situations:

- May you too be free from the burdens you are experiencing.
- May you be free from sorrow and grief.
- May you receive the support you need to heal.
- May life rise up to meet you exactly where you are.
- May you be well and live your life with ease.

As we worked together and I supported her ongoing meditation practice, Lydia gained insight into her own wounded heart. Her father had died early of alcoholism, and her mother had been deeply depressed. Through diligent meditation practice and psychotherapy, Lydia began to make peace with the hurt child she had once been. She joined Adult Children of Alcoholics, which in conjunction with the other inner work she did, gradually allowed her to heal. By recognizing her own injury and by having made friends with the wounded child within herself, she discovered her own potential to be a wounded healer. Eventually she became a support and sponsor for other parents of children with drug addictions.

Gradually it became possible for Lydia to feel empathy and warmth for Tina again. The Breathing Through Meditation also allowed Lydia to stay open to her daughter's suffering without being overwhelmed by it. When beginning this meditation, Lydia remembered her interconnectedness with the web of life. She prayed,

- As my breath continues in its effortless flow, I visualize breath as a stream, a breath-stream that touches me gently.

Then, while holding an image of the struggling Tina in her mind's eye, she continued,

- As I extend my awareness outward beyond myself to the suffering that is present in Tina's life,
- I allow my protective walls to drop.
- I allow images of Tina to come forward, images of her fear and isolation.

- I open to images of wounding and damage in wider and wider circles of family suffering, and I allow myself to relax and just let them surface.

She closed with,

- As the breath-stream flows through, I imagine the out-breath touching the open weave of my heart, carrying in its flow the pain of others.
- And as I experience myself as part of the interconnected flow of life, I feel secure, alive, and fully awake.

This meditation has remained part of Lydia's regular practice to this day, while Tina continues to struggle with addiction.

Key Points

- Developing compassion for yourself allows you to extend compassion to others.
- With ongoing practice, your ability to feel compassion and offer it to others increases.
- Compassion can expand in a widening spiral, leading from yourself, to others, and to the world.
- Your own woundedness can lead to a widened space within your own heart, allowing you to feel compassion for others and become engaged on behalf of those who suffer in this world.

⟶ COMPASSION FOR OTHERS PRACTICE

- May I tend to you during this trying time with loving care.
- May I offer you compassion, especially when you feel vulnerable.
- May I extend caring toward you, especially when you feel scared and lonely.

- May I be present with you when fear leads you to contract and shut down.
- May I meet you with gentleness and friendship.
- May I recognize your sense of shame, guilt, and insecurity with gentle understanding and respect.
- May I be aware that you and I are both part of the interdependent field of wisdom and compassion.
- May you be free from suffering and the causes of suffering.
- May you receive the support you need.
- May life rise up to meet us all.

⟿ BREATHING THROUGH MEDITATION (ADAPTED FROM JOANNA MACY)

- I make myself comfortable and feel the touch of my seat.
- I let my awareness descend into my body, right down to the ground.
- I bring my awareness to these sensations of firmness and solidity.
- With a quiet mind, an attentive mind, I am simply present within my body while allowing for a sense of ease.
- I settle my breathing in its natural rhythm, in its effortless flow.
- With every out-breath I release tension and let thoughts or memories pass by.
- I continue to relax all the way through the out-breath.
- I let go even beyond the end of the out-breath while the next breath flows in effortlessly.
- I inhale as naturally as I exhale, just letting my body breathe.
- As my breath continues in its effortless flow, I visualize breath as a breath-stream that touches me tenderly, and as I gently bring my awareness to the area of my heart, I imagine the breath-stream touching my heart delicately while flowing through.

- As I continue to allow breath to breathe through me, I extend my awareness outward to the suffering that is present in life.
- I allow my protective walls to drop as I open to the knowledge of suffering.
- I allow images to come forward, of people in fear and isolation.
- I open to images of wounding in wider and wider circles of suffering.
- I relax and just let them surface.
- Then I allow one specific image to come forward.
- There might be one person or animal I am worried about.
- I pause and slowly take in as much detail as I can.
- And as I offer the hospitality of my presence and my attention to this wounded one, I pause again and notice what I am experiencing.
- Noticing where I feel this suffering in my body, I gently bring my attention back to the flow of my breath.
- And as the breath-stream flows through, I imagine the out-breath touching the open weave of my heart, carrying in its flow the pain of this being.
- I know that all I have to do is to allow this to happen, for the breath-stream to touch my and others' hearts.
- So I loosen my heart and allow the breath-stream to flow through.

JOURNAL EXERCISE

Sit down with a pencil and paper in a quiet place. Make yourself comfortable, rest in your gentle breath, and see what images and stories arise as you read the following prompts. If your own experiences come to mind, do some free writing.

1. Describe a time in your life when it was hard for you to call up compassion for a friend, relative, or colleague.
2. If you were able to find compassion for this person, describe how you accessed it and what happened when you expressed it.
3. If you are currently struggling to find compassion for somebody in your life, do some free writing about all the thoughts and feelings that come up. Allow this writing to carry you wherever it will.
4. Write a possible scenario about what might happen if you were able to access your compassion for this person. Describe how you may see the person and engage differently with him or her.

12

The Heart That Cares for All (Bodhichitta) Practice

The Heart That Cares for All (Bodhichitta) Practice teaches you to cultivate the deep wish to wake up for the benefit of all beings. In Buddhism, a person on the bodhisattva path is living an intention to engage with the world with wide and inclusive compassion, a heart that cares for all life. As your compassion for yourself becomes stronger and your capacity to be present with suffering and pain deepens, you can motivate yourself to open your heart in an ever-widening arc of caring— for yourself, for others who suffer, and for our struggling world. As you strengthen your metaphorical heart muscle, you may find yourself longing above all else that all beings are safe, well, and free. As this attitude becomes part of your personality, compassion manifests in your life as a natural, spontaneous way of responding. With the Heart That Cares for All Practice, you express and cultivate your deepest yearning for the well-being of all life.

The heart that cares for all provides the foundation for your compassionate actions. "The desire for the welfare of all beings becomes our foundation stone," says the Buddhist scholar and social activist Joanna

Macy. "We can think of it as a flame in our hearts and minds that guides us and shines through our actions."[13]

His Holiness the Dalai Lama emphasizes over and over that bodhichitta originates from your understanding and experience of the interconnectedness of all beings. Your own health and well-being cannot be separated from the health and well-being of everyone else. The potential to express this heart that cares for all is always present within you, yet you may not be aware of it. Therefore, you need to pay attention to this potential. By developing a practice to cultivate your bigheartedness, you choose to follow its calling.

You may worry that the motivation to include all beings in your caring demands too much of you. However, a wide and caring heart is not a "should" or an obligation, but a longing that awakens naturally. The more your heart opens, whether this is through your meditation practice or experiences of caring, the more you yearn to live a life that is filled with a feeling of love.

You might say, "I can't think about all beings, as I have a hard enough time in taking care of myself and my family." And yes, it is easier to feel compassion for those close to you. But you are asked to expand your capacity to care for others gently and gradually. We have to "inch ourselves forward" and start with small steps. Diligent and compassionate cultivation of your ability to be inclusive makes it possible for you to go beyond your immediate comfort zone to tap into a hidden capacity that has been available to you all along. Rewards are great, as expanding your ability to care can leave you with more confidence in and respect for yourself and can contribute to your inner happiness, as well as that of others, in a lasting way.

So many of us have lost access to our innate good-heartedness. Joanna Macy describes this condition as "wounded bodhichitta." Being scared, overwhelmed, or badly hurt can leave your capacity for boundless love badly damaged. For example, having suffered great pain in your life may have left you hardened and led you to close off from the world. You may be filled with self-loathing and anger. Difficult life experiences can undermine your ability to love. As you begin to address the painful underground currents from the past, you slowly make your way out of being stuck and focused on yourself. To free yourself may then seem more possible.

With true self-compassion and the help of empathic and insightful teachers and therapists, you can gradually move from self-loathing to self-compassion and eventually to compassion for all. The Self-Compassion, Compassion for Others, and Heart That Cares for All practices may not only benefit the world; they can also be powerful healing tools for your own wounded heart.

There is a Buddhist story about the "spoonful of salt effect." If you put a spoonful of salt into a glass of water, the water ends up being very salty. If you put the spoonful of salt into a lake, then the water will not be salty at all. This means if you stay stuck with your pain in a small container of self-preoccupation, you will most likely suffer more severely.

However, if you open up to others despite your own wounds and include others in your caring, your experience of your own pain diminishes. You can experience yourself as part of a wider and more fluid field. A wounded healer is a person whose accepting relationship to his or her own suffering has become the inspiration to assist others in their recovery. In this way, he or she has allowed pain to be a gateway for becoming a healer to others who suffer.

MICHAEL'S STORY

Practicing bigheartedness is essential to my husband, Michael, in his life's work. He is a hospice doctor who works with people who are dying as well as with their stressed and grieving families. The Heart That Cares for All Practice supports him when he sees himself confronted with situations that seem unfixable, when healing is needed, but there is no cure. I asked Michael if he could tell me a story of how he transformed his dedication to live in the spirit of bodhichitta into a deliberate practice for himself.

Looking at me pensively, he began, "In the mornings I start by connecting my meditations to the well-being of others. I do that to expand the circle of those I wish well to as much as I can. I finish my morning meditations with a bodhichitta prayer, which is my way of holding the possibility for boundless caring in my consciousness. It goes like this:

- May all beings be happy.
- May all beings be safe.
- May all beings be free.
- May I become what I need to become to best enable this to happen.

Then Michael told me that he regularly dedicates his meditations to the well-being of all life. When he walks into very difficult and painful situations with his patients, he practices bigheartedness. After being lost in thought for a moment, he told me the following story: "Recently I had heard from the nurses that there was a family whose members were furiously blaming each other. I was to go in and talk to the two sisters and the brother about their dying mother. The three adult siblings were already struggling over the considerable inheritance to come. The conflicts over their future inheritance impacted the way each sister considered possible treatment plans. The oldest sister was controlling the situation, as she was the mother's guardian. I knew that I had to discuss the further treatment plan with the three of them and was worried about possible conflict."

As Michael shared his worries about this family, I asked, "How did you calm the family down enough so that they could listen to each other's point of view? I would have been frightened to go into a meeting with them."

The morning of the planned family meeting, Michael went into the hospital chapel. He knew that he had about ten minutes to connect to himself. He realized that it was fear that caused his heart to feel constricted and that his feeling of trepidation made it hard for him to experience openness toward the troubled family. Since he knew that the heart that cares for all is an antidote to fear, he chose the Dissolving Fear in Bodhichitta Practice.

⌾ DISSOLVING FEAR IN BODHICHITTA PRACTICE

- I notice the sensations of fear in my body.
- I recognize how much discomfort I am experiencing.
- I choose to pause the cycle of suffering, and feel the gentle breath of my heart.
- I offer compassion to myself, and stay with the felt sense of my own suffering.
- I notice the current of fear passing by, like a cold wind brushing through the winter streets, and I let this storm pass by, without grasping or pushing away.
- I remember that all of us are afraid and that all of us want to be free.
- Just as I am committed to waking up and finding freedom, I include the well-being and freedom of all in my care.
- May all beings, humans and animals, be released from fear and trepidation. May we be happy and free.
- I ground myself in the sensation of breath, in the flow of life that connects us all.

Michael told me that after doing this practice, he felt stronger and increasingly calm. He felt held by a sense of interbeing, and as a result, he felt less scared.

Slowly and mindfully, he walked up to the ward. Before entering the family conference room, he stood for a minute at the big window in the hospital hallway, sensing his feet on the ground. He looked out at a big chestnut tree, marveling at how the sun hit the beautiful leaves. There he stood, taking three conscious breaths. With each out-breath, he included a wish for all those in pain. "Then I was able to remind myself that this was not about me and that there is a wider perspective," he noted. "In that moment I dedicated my fear and discomfort to the well-being of others, the family suffering here, but also to all the human people, the animal people, the plants, and our earth."

Michael explained that letting the pain flow through, instead of holding what was painful too tightly, was crucial for him. "The contracted energy needs to loosen up. So I let it flow through me, like water coming down, flowing between the rocks of a stream. Rather than letting the suffering gather and get stuck in my chest, I allowed it to flow through me for the sake of all beings."

As he stood there, feeling the soft breath moving through his body, he began to feel less alone. He began to experience himself as part of the web of life: "I suddenly felt faith that the wisdom and compassion necessary would arise spontaneously to save this encounter. It was as if I were trusting that grace would happen. Energetically, this dedication to the well-being of all allowed the energy to flow through me, and as I let go, the energy was no longer trapped. Otherwise, I would have gone in there all stuck and armored up as I met with that distraught family."

When Michael met the angry siblings in the conference room, he was able to be present with them. Staying connected with the felt sense in his body, he was able to see the fear lurking behind their anger and attempts to control the situation. His equanimity and presence allowed the three siblings to refocus on their mother and on the realities of her care needs. Because Michael felt less frightened and contracted in his own heart, the siblings could let down their guard as well. The atmosphere in the room had warmed up just enough to allow for the necessary opening in communication to happen.

When you open yourself to the stream of all suffering beings, you are less defensive toward others. Then you are not engaging from the perspective of your ego, of what suits you at that moment, but on behalf of life.

In our conversation, Michael explained how "healing is not something that we personally do to or for another. Healing is what naturally happens when we (the other and I) become part of the fluid, interconnected, impermanent, always changing process that is reality." This is an essential insight of the Heart That Cares for All Practice. "In that way," Michael said, "it is no longer a matter of congratulating ourselves when things go well or blaming ourselves when they don't. We do our best. We contribute to the process. Then something happens that is ultimately not in our control. What is in our power is to set our deepest and widest intention, choose to do what we think is in the best interest of the other, and let go of outcome."

Michael values most that we are aware of the interconnectedness of all things, that we cultivate the conditions for healing within ourselves and in our relationship with the suffering of others. He concluded by saying, "Together, we wait to see what emerges."

He told me that the Heart That Cares for All Practice especially helps him when he feels discouraged and overwhelmed by his work. "During those times, I often don't know anymore what is up and what is down, what is important in life. Then I just want to hide. This practice helps me to become clear again about who I am. Then I know once more what I am here to contribute. Interestingly enough, when I clarify my purpose and intention, then I also feel physically much more animated and resilient and ready to open the door to my next patient."

Key Points

- The heart that cares for all is the deep longing to wake up for the well-being of all life.
- When you dedicate your life's work to a bigger context, this brings you more happiness and meaning.
- When you focus on the Heart That Cares for All Practice, it will give a wider and more meaningful direction to your life.
- When you cultivate a Heart That Cares for All Practice, your heart's capacity to feel love and offer spontaneous compassion grows.

⌐ THE HEART THAT CARES FOR ALL (BODHICHITTA) PRACTICE

- I let myself come to a state of relaxation and stillness.
- I notice my body with quiet alertness.

- I notice the subtle flow of breath for my body to be breathed.
- Now I allow myself to cultivate a deeply caring heart, and the wish to become fully awake and alive, for my sake and that of all beings.
- I notice my longing for freedom, for being fully awake and alive, and for my life to have meaning and purpose.
- I follow my breath with quiet alertness.
- We all are part of the interconnected web of life, affecting those around us.
- I ask myself, *What would I most love to offer the world?*
- I ask myself, *What would I like to share in terms of skills, gifts?*
- I ask myself, *What talent of mine would be my best contribution?*
- With each breath, I let my breath join the breath of the world.
- With each breath, I feel my connection with all life and sense all our interdependence.
- With each breath, I allow myself to be porous and fluid, open to life's energy.
- With each in-breath and out-breath, I envision myself sharing my talents with our world.
- As I feel the gentle breath, I offer loving-kindness to all beings.
- I imagine sharing my gifts with others, contributing to the world becoming a better place.
- With each breath, I connect to humans, animals, and our world, to beings that live now and beings that will inhabit our world in the future.
- I notice the subtle flow of breath, for all of life to be breathed.

⇒ DISSOLVING FEAR IN BODHICHITTA PRACTICE

- I notice the sensations of fear in my body. I choose to pause the cycle of suffering.
- I feel the gentle breath of my heart and my feet touching the ground.

- I offer compassion to myself and stay with the felt sense of my pain.
- I notice the current of fear passing by, like a cold wind brushing through the winter streets.
- I let this storm move through, without grasping or pushing away.
- I remember that all of us are afraid and that all of us want to be free.
- Just as I am committed to waking up and finding freedom, I include in my care the well-being and freedom of others.
- May we all—humans, animals, and our earth—be free from suffering and the causes of suffering.
- May we all receive the support we need, and may we grant it to each other.
- I ground myself in the sensation of breath and surrender to its wisdom.

⤙ AN ON-THE-GO HEART-THAT-CARES-FOR-ALL PRACTICE

(Twenty-second practice)

- May all beings be happy.
- May all beings be safe.
- May all beings be free.
- May my longing be to contribute to the well-being and freedom of others.
- May I receive the support to make this happen.
- May wisdom, compassion, and abundant generosity manifest in my actions.

JOURNAL EXERCISE

Sit down with a pencil and paper in a quiet place. Make yourself comfortable, rest in your gentle breath, and see what images and stories arise as you read the following prompts. If your own experiences come to mind, do some free writing.

1. Write about a time in your life when you have been caught, as we all are at times, in your own small story.
2. Can you remember another time when you opened your story up to include the well-being of others? Write about that.
3. Think of a time when you wanted to open your heart to the well-being of others and were unable to do that. Write your own story of wounded bodhichitta.
4. Now imagine how your story could have unfolded if you had been able to act in the spirit of the heart that cares for all. Be bold when you imagine!

13

The Compassionate Choice Practice

His Holiness the Dalai Lama tells us, "Although you may not be able to avoid difficult situations, you can modify the extent to which you (and others) suffer by how you choose to respond to the situation."[14] One way you can show your compassionate attitude is by working with your difficult emotions. The Compassionate Choice Practice will help you to bring mindfulness and compassion to times when something has incited an angry, fearful, embarrassed, or otherwise difficult response. You might say that you have been triggered.

If you face a complex or painfully recurring pattern in your life, then seeing clearly what is going on is crucial. The Compassionate Choice Practice allows you to slow down, infuse awareness into the reactive process, pause, consider your possible responses from a wider perspective, and then gradually choose a more healing response. In a systematic way this practice helps you to identify what triggered you, the sensations and emotions you are experiencing as a result, and how what is happening in the present moment connects you to events from the past.

During a six-week professional training course seven years ago, I had settled comfortably into a particular chair in the conference hall and claimed it each day. One morning, about two weeks into the course, I was surprised to see that another participant had taken over my chair and had moved all my things to the back of the room. I was outraged; my shoulders and jaw were tense; I was triggered. Old memories from my childhood surfaced, and familiar feelings of rejection and being invisible surfaced.

Unconscious beliefs about yourself or life in general may have been fueling *long-standing recurrent painful patterns* (LRPPs, pronounced *lerps*) of how you experience situations. Some of those patterns may have been asleep in your psyche for a long time but are stirred up by a specific trigger. It helps to not only recognize what triggered you, but also to discern your old patterns, your particular underlying "propensity to be bothered." As old patterns of relating often entangle you in hurtful ways, it is a relief to free yourself from them.

My LRPP in the situation at the professional training course was my propensity to feel rejected and excluded and to feel terribly hurt whenever something like that happened again. I felt the takeover of my chair as a personal rebuff and as an example that once more I was not accepted in a group.

Driven to relieve discomfort, you may act impulsively to fix an upsetting feeling. Sometimes you might "act out," meaning that you might behave in ways that are hurtful towards others or yourself in obvious and noticeable ways. At other times, you might do what I call "act in," which involves becoming consumed with self-criticism. These thoughts and feelings turn inward in painful ways.

In the conference hall, I fantasized about confronting the person who had taken over my seat and "reconquering my chair." At the same time, I felt embarrassed about feeling so upset about this minor incident and criticized myself harshly.

The Compassionate Choice Practice includes taking a Mindful Time-Out, which can prevent a painful process from cascading toward reactive behavior and allow you to find your balance again. Taking a second look at a problematic situation with a clearer mind and heart allows you to develop and hold a wiser perspective. In the Compassionate Choice Practice, by choosing to pause, you can develop your capacity for loving awareness, self-acceptance, and understanding, especially when facing feelings such as resentment, shame, or depressive hopelessness.

Luckily I realized that I had been triggered at the training course and that my inner turbulence was about to cascade down in destructive ways. I decided to take a Mindful Time-Out, to walk for a while in the neighboring fields and then meditate in my room. I was instantly able to realize that old painful patterns from my past had become inflamed again. I could look at myself with compassion, which allowed me to take a wider perspective and communicate skillfully. With a new perspective and a good conversation, I also understood that the other participant was elderly and had not been able to hear the speaker from her old place in the back. We added another chair close to where I was sitting so we both would have good spots to see and hear the speakers.

By connecting the events that have happened in the present moment to those from the past, you will gain insight into how you have become stuck. Understanding leads to compassion. With deeper insight, you can find your way forward in a skillful, compassionate way and gain a wider perspective even in complex situations. This will help you to make a mindful and compassionate choice. The following chart shows the steps in the Compassionate Choice Practice. The Compassionate Choice Practice consists of three parts. The first part allows you to notice when you have been triggered. You usually perceive this as a physical, cognitive, and emotional event. The middle part of the practice asks you to take a Mindful Time-Out, a time of respite and rebalance, which you can tailor to your needs. A Mindful Time-Out helps you to regain a sense of calm and groundedness. The third part of the practice guides you to find a new attitude and a skillful way of responding. You may first take a compassionate look at yourself and view your situation from a wider perspective. Doing so will help you to make wise and compassionate choices.

Compassionate Choice Practice

TRIGGER
Something happens that sparks an immediate uncomfortable feeling. This trigger can be set off by internal thoughts and feelings or by external events.

SENSATION
Our body responds instantaneously. We may experience, for example, a tightening in our belly, a constriction near our heart, or a flushed face.

EMOTION
Feelings that come up may be anger, fear, sadness, embarrassment, indignation, or some other unpleasant emotion.

AUTOMATIC ASSOCIATION
Moods, memories, and images from our past arise and entangle us and intensify emotions.

EMOTIONAL CONCLUSION
Consciously or unconsciously, we form beliefs about ourselves, others, and our world which seem convincing.

URGE TO ACT
We experience a great deal of tension, which can be externalized as an intense desire to fix the situation or internalized as intense rumination.

Mindful Time-Out

We choose to interrupt the reactive process with an activity that restores our inner balance. We notice the sensations and emotions of more tenderness and quiet.

COMPASSIONATE AWARENESS
We notice our reaction to the trigger with compassion for ourselves and others.

SENSATIONS & EMOTIONS OF COMPASSION
We feel the sensations and emotions when expanding our care to ourselves and others.

COMPASSIONATE EVALUATION
We gain a wider perspective and can consider a range of possibilities.

COMPASSIONATE CHOICE
We respond with more awareness, skill, and care.

RESULTING SENSATIONS & EMOTIONS
We feel the sensations and emotions having made a compassionate choice. We may feel increased relaxation, physical wellness, aliveness, and an improved connection with others.

OUTCOME
New response patterns can develop and our relationship to ourselves and others improve.

A model worksheet allows you to fill in the steps as they unfold. By filling in the Compassionate Choice Practice Worksheet, you can see with clear eyes how you got entangled in a problematic situation. For your convenience, you can work the Compassionate Choice Practice on paper or in its digital version on the website Mindfulpause.org.

Compassionate Choice Practice Worksheet

TRIGGER

SENSATION

EMOTION

AUTOMATIC ASSOCIATION

EMOTIONAL CONCLUSION

URGE TO ACT

Mindful Time-Out

COMPASSIONATE AWARENESS

SENSATIONS & EMOTIONS OF COMPASSION

COMPASSIONATE EVALUATION

COMPASSIONATE CHOICE

RESULTING SENSATIONS & EMOTIONS

OUTCOME

HENRY'S STORY

Henry, the graduate student who was introduced in Chapter 7, faced new challenges several years later after he received his doctorate when he applied for a position as a professor at different universities. He had married a woman who had immigrated to the United States from China five years earlier. In short succession, they had two children, a boy and a girl. Henry was the sole breadwinner in his young family.

Henry had been doing Mindfulness Meditation and Loving Awareness Practices somewhat regularly for six years. Meditation and psychotherapy had helped him deal with his considerable anxiety as well as his tendency to be obsessive and a bit suspicious. One Monday morning when he came to our session, Henry seemed quite upset. He was under great pressure to find permanent work. Stressed by a job interview with Professor R., Henry was suffering from anxiety, especially when he woke up during the night. He reported that he had felt triggered when Prof. R. ended a recent phone interview in a way that Henry interpreted as "abrupt." With pleading eyes, Henry asked me to help him find relief from feeling "so stressed" and afraid that he would never be able to feed his family.

After I listened carefully to Henry's experience, I asked him if he would be open to allowing me to guide him through the Compassionate Choice Practice. I had a hunch that this practice might help him at a time when he was feeling thrown off balance and upset.

I showed him the worksheet, and we filled out each of the steps together.

TRIGGER

SENSATION

EMOTION

AUTOMATIC ASSOCIATION

EMOTIONAL CONCLUSION

URGE TO ACT

Trigger

A trigger is an internal or external event that often sets off a cascade of your sensory, emotional, and cognitive experiences and behavioral reactions.

Henry's entry: "I felt set off by the abrupt ending of the phone call and the uncertainty following this contact with Professor R."

Sensations

Tactile sensations are your gateway to the present moment and signify the impact the event has on you.

Henry's entry: "During and immediately after the phone call, I experienced tension in my neck and shoulders. I also had a knot in my stomach and was not able to sleep that night."

Emotions

Emotions are often experienced together or in close time connection with physical sensations and thoughts. Emotions, sensations, and thoughts bring intensity to your experience.

Henry's entry: "I felt extraordinarily anxious and worried about my future. I feared that I was not going to get this or any other job."

Automatic Associations

Automatic associations are involuntary, showing up as moods, memories, or images that link the current event to the past while heightening and seemingly entangling your emotional states.

Henry's entry: "My experience became increasingly complicated as a barrage of images and memories followed. I felt haunted by memories of my father criticizing, ridiculing, and belittling me, even though I was now an accomplished research scientist at a prestigious university. I felt completely surprised how many old feelings were hovering behind this recent experience with Professor R."

Emotional Conclusion

Unconsciously, emotionally charged beliefs may have slumbered in your psyche and been painfully awakened by the cascading internal process following the trigger.

Henry's entry: "I realized that I had unknowingly labeled myself in a detrimental way—as a failure. I judged my response to Professor R. as a mistake and felt that I was not good enough for this or any other job. I also worried about being inadequate as a father, husband, and son."

Urge to Act

Often this snowballing process leads to an urge to act, a desire to fix the uncomfortable situation at hand and relieve the tension by reacting internally or externally.

Henry's entry: "In response to experiencing myself as a failure, I felt a strong urge to write angry e-mails to Professor R. I even considered issuing a preemptive refusal of this job. I felt paralyzed by my fear and had to fight the temptation to hide in bed, continuously ruminating about my imperfections."

It was lucky that Henry had come in to therapy before sending a letter to Professor R. "It's amazing how rapidly I become reactive," he commented. "I sure will do this worksheet before sending any more letters to future employers." Then he asked, "But what can I do now?"

I told Henry about the Mindful Time-Out, which would allow him to interrupt his reactivity and find balance again: "After you have regained your balance a bit, I will teach you to look at yourself with more kindness and to see a wider perspective so you can make a wiser choice in the future."

Then Henry filled out the second part of the chart, Mindful Time-Out.

Mindful Time-Out

┌───┐
│   │
│   │
│   │
└───┘

Mindful Time-Out

A Mindful Time-Out increases your capacity to step off the chain of reactivity. There are a number of necessary conditions for this to happen, such as recognizing the reactive chain of events. By cultivating a background state of calm and clear-minded presence, you can choose how to proceed mindfully.

Henry's entry: "I asked Radhule if she could guide me in a 20-minute meditation, hoping that this would help me to feel more calm, collected and clear-headed again. After this short meditation I was ready to continue calmly and skillfully with the second half of the Compassionate Choice Practice."

After Henry had regained his composure and balance with the support of the Mindful Time-Out, he was now ready to engage in the third part of the chart.

COMPASSIONATE AWARENESS

┌───┐
│   │
│   │
│   │
└───┘

SENSATIONS & EMOTIONS OF COMPASSION

┌───┐
│   │
│   │
│   │
└───┘

COMPASSIONATE EVALUATION

┌───┐
│   │
│   │
│   │
└───┘

COMPASSIONATE CHOICE

RESULTING SENSATIONS & EMOTIONS

OUTCOME

Compassionate Awareness

Compassionate awareness allows you to meet all your experiences with self-compassion.

Henry's entry: "Now I was able to see my internal experiences clearly and to regard my thoughts and feelings with self-empathy. Memories of feeling frightened by my father's ridicule and anger helped me to feel more understanding and tender toward myself. As I felt kinder toward myself, I was able to relax and see things in a more discerning and hopeful way.

Compassionate Evaluation

Feeling less fearful and constricted, you can evaluate a situation anew and thus hold a wider perspective.

Henry's entry: "Finally I realized that there might have been many other reasons for Professor R.'s abrupt interruption of the phone call. I even wondered if his wife might have wanted to go out for dinner: it was Friday at 5:00 P.M. after all! I also reminded myself of the fact that I had several other job interviews lined up and that this was not my only chance of getting a job.

Compassionate Choice

With more awareness and skill, you can respond differently, which may include skillful actions or, alternatively, a wise discernment to abstain from reactive behavior.

Henry's entry: "I am choosing to abstain from sending more e-mails to Professor R. My practice is to be aware of my full range of feelings as they pass through my body and psyche and to do so as compassionately as possible. I also realized that I had given my father and his stand-in, Professor R., too much power. As they shrank back to size in my mind, I became less anxious.

One year later, I received a letter from Henry, who had moved with his family and was now living close to his new university appointment. He had included in his letter the entries for the last two steps in the Compassionate Choice Practice. The last two steps of the Compassionate Choice Practice allow you to recognize the "resulting sensations and emotions as well as the "outcome," the positive impact of this practice on a challenging situation.

Resulting Sensations and Emotions

With ongoing practice, old habit patterns can change, leading to more freedom and happiness.

Henry's entry: "I realize that I have become more content and happier over time. I feel stronger and more settled in myself. Now I experience far fewer periods of anxiety. With a continuous practice of exercise, meditation, and occasional meetings with a psychotherapist at my new place of employment, I have begun to feel increasingly solid. I am able to prevent future episodes of entrenched anxiety and depression. When occasional challenges come up, periods of anxious feelings pass quickly. My life feels lighter now."

Using the Compassionate Choice Practice, Henry learned to bring mindfulness to difficult moments. He was increasingly able to track when triggers occurred, to condition himself to take a Mindful Time-Out and to become more *responsive* rather than *reactive* in his life. This in turn helped him to bring awareness to the process of being triggered. Neuropsychiatrist Dan Siegel tells us, "Even when one looks in hindsight at unfortunate events, awareness opens up situations and introduces the possibility of choice and change and eventually to the creation of new habitual pathways, even neural pathways."[15]

Outcome

With ongoing practice, new habits can develop, which may correspond to lasting physiological changes in the brain.

Henry's entry: "Our family finally moved to my new place of work. I know that I need to keep practicing so that I can develop fresh, mindful habits and a gentler attitude toward myself."

Key Points

- The Compassionate Choice Practice helps you to recognize when you have been triggered and to work with those situations more skillfully.
- Having an ongoing practice helps you to recognize more easily when something has thrown you out of balance.
- The Compassionate Choice Practice allows you to understand clearly and swiftly the complex dimensions of your predicament.
- Understanding how past experiences may have made you vulnerable to present experiences leads to compassion.
- The Mindful Time-Out allows you to choose a pause in which you are able to rebalance yourself.
- The compassionate choice allows for a wise and skillful way of going forward.
- The Compassionate Choice Practice allows you to gain a wider perspective.
- The Compassionate Choice Practice can be successfully combined with the Mindful Pause Practice or one of the Mindfulness On-the-Go practices from Chapter 15.

Compassionate Choice Practice

TRIGGER
Something happens that sparks an immediate uncomfortable feeling. This trigger can be set off by internal thoughts and feelings or by external events.

SENSATION
Our body responds instantaneously. We may experience, for example, a tightening in our belly, a constriction near our heart, or a flushed face.

EMOTION
Feelings that come up may be anger, fear, sadness, embarrassment, indignation, or some other unpleasant emotion.

AUTOMATIC ASSOCIATION
Moods, memories, and images from our past arise and entangle us and intensify emotions.

EMOTIONAL CONCLUSION
Consciously or unconsciously, we form beliefs about ourselves, others, and our world which seem convincing.

URGE TO ACT
We experience a great deal of tension, which can be externalized as an intense desire to fix the situation or internalized as intense rumination.

Mindful Time-Out

We choose to interrupt the reactive process with an activity that restores our inner balance. We notice the sensations and emotions of more tenderness and quiet.

COMPASSIONATE AWARENESS
We notice our reaction to the trigger with compassion for ourselves and others.

SENSATIONS & EMOTIONS OF COMPASSION
We feel the sensations and emotions when expanding our care to ourselves and others.

COMPASSIONATE EVALUATION
We gain a wider perspective and can consider a range of possibilities.

COMPASSIONATE CHOICE
We respond with more awareness, skill, and care.

RESULTING SENSATIONS & EMOTIONS
We feel the sensations and emotions having made a compassionate choice. We may feel increased relaxation, physical wellness, aliveness, and an improved connection with others.

OUTCOME
New response patterns can develop and our relationship to ourselves and others improve.

Compassionate Choice Practice Worksheet

TRIGGER

SENSATION

EMOTION

AUTOMATIC ASSOCIATION

EMOTIONAL CONCLUSION

URGE TO ACT

Mindful Time-Out

COMPASSIONATE AWARENESS

SENSATIONS & EMOTIONS OF COMPASSION

COMPASSIONATE EVALUATION

COMPASSIONATE CHOICE

RESULTING SENSATIONS & EMOTIONS

OUTCOME

JOURNAL EXERCISE

Sit down with a pencil and paper in a quiet place. Make yourself comfortable, rest in your gentle breath, and see what images and stories arise as you read the following prompts. If your own experiences come to mind, do some free writing.

1. Describe a time when you have been triggered, even if it was only by a small event.
2. See if there is an underlying belief or thought pattern that leads you to react in familiar ways over and over. Do some free writing.
3. With your example, go through the steps of the Compassionate Choice Practice chart. If you have not done so yet, take a Mindful Time-Out. Then envision a more skillful response to your trigger. Notice how you feel at the end of the exercise.

14

The Spiral of Compassion and Forgiveness Practice

The Spiral of Compassion and Forgiveness is a step-by-step practice that will help you face and work through a conflict you have experienced in the past. It can help you particularly when you have encountered a hurtful situation with another person and feel thrown off balance. You may have felt hurt, angry, misunderstood, or disappointed, or thought you were betrayed or otherwise treated unfairly. Or perhaps you are carrying the weight of having acted in ways you later regretted, so that you are in conflict with yourself.

By using the Spiral of Compassion and Forgiveness Practice, you are shifting the center of gravity of your awareness into your heart—your center of feeling and psychospiritual perception. When you view the world from your heart, you are literally looking from a new perspective.

The Spiral of Compassion and Forgiveness Practice offers a skillful alternative to the Compassionate Choice Practice discussed in Chapter 13. In the Compassionate Choice Practice, the emphasis is on making skillful choices by noticing and understanding your inner process and the roots of your conflicts step-by-step. In a struggle, where you may have felt painfully disappointed by someone, you could have worked through the problem with the help of the Compassionate Choice Practice Worksheet. A deeper understanding may have helped you to make more skillful choices or to abstain from destructive actions, such as sending scathing e-mails or talking badly about the person you have the problem with. Understanding may have led to compassion.

On the other hand, the Spiral of Compassion and Forgiveness Practice emphasizes learning to experience from a heart place from which you see the world with new and tender eyes. By tapping into your heart, you also have a chance to experience the felt sense of compassion, forgiveness, acceptance, and gratitude. Forgiveness especially allows you to let go of the burden of any resentments you hold. You have the opportunity to surrender to the present moment, which allows your heart's intuition to come forth. Then love, wisdom, and creativity can emerge together and spontaneously.

⤚ THE SPIRAL OF COMPASSION AND FOREGIVENESS PRACTICE

1. I dedicate this practice to a purpose or an intention.
2. I focus my attention with Mindfulness Meditation.
3. I turn my gaze inward to see what is going on inside.
4. I extend compassion toward myself or hold the intention to do so when I am ready.
5. I offer forgiveness to myself or hold the intention to do so when I am ready.
6. I offer acceptance for who I am right now in my life.
7. I extend compassion toward all those who experience suffering similar to mine.
8. I extend compassion toward those with whom I have a problem or hold the intention to do so when I am ready.
9. I set the intention to extend forgiveness toward those with whom I have a problem, and, if I am ready, I offer them forgiveness.

10. If possible, I open my heart in acceptance of my relationship as it is right now.
11. I extend well-wishing and loving-kindness toward all beings.
12. I extend gratitude for being able work through my challenges and thankfulness that we all have the opportunity to be free.

I recommend that you complete this process by dedicating the benefits of doing this work to all other beings and the world.

When you have been in conflict with another person, the Spiral of Compassion and Forgiveness Practice can help you to feel deep inside yourself and experience your emotional injuries. Leaning into your own disappointment and sorrow can allow you to generate an inner feeling of compassion and forgiveness. Ultimately it may lead you to accept the truth of your situation. Maybe you will understand that both you and the problematic other have been hurt and are afraid. Maybe you will understand that both of you have experienced feelings of abandonment. Doing so can paved an easier path to forgiveness.

In the twelve-step process of the Spiral of Compassion and Forgiveness Practice, you work with intention setting, focusing, and turning inward in a gentle way. This practice gives you guidelines on how to work with your wounded feelings. By offering compassion, forgiveness, and acceptance to others as well as to yourself, you will be able to let go of old worries and find peace. Forgiveness will ultimately allow you to let go of old burdens, such as bitterness, resentment, or even rage. Softening, and maybe even healing old wounds, allows you to open your heart to both the joy and the suffering of our world.

As I have worked my way through my inner turmoil many times, it has struck me that compassion, forgiveness, and acceptance toward others and myself often moves in a spiral-like fashion. When you gently and respectfully address your difficult feelings toward yourself and others, you will eventually be able to experience true relief. Then you can learn to reclaim your life energy and share your love with the rest of the world.

STEVEN'S AND MY STORY

Some years ago, my friend Steven and I were giving a seminar on Jungian dream work together. Steven and I prided ourselves on how well we were working as a team, even though our styles were very different. His strengths were structure and precise articulation, while mine were in group facilitation and the promotion of direct experience. I was aware that Steven was under a lot of stress due to a recent crisis in his family—his brother had died unexpectedly. I was worried that this would affect our goal to work smoothly together.

One day our differences got the better of us, and feelings of competitiveness and irritation became obvious. As we were working with the group, I felt cut short by Steven several times. He interrupted me on numerous occasions and twice ridiculed my approach, in front of others, for being too soft and emotionally cathartic. As the course continued over the following weeks, the situation did not improve. My old pattern of feeling rejected and criticized was activated. I knew that Steven was in a vulnerable state, but I could not help but feel offended by his attitude. After one seminar, Steven criticized a piece of my work with a group member. I felt deeply hurt. It seemed to me as if he saw his own way of teaching as intellectually superior. When I got home that night, I shot a message out, asking Steven to change his attitude. He, in turn, experienced this as disapproval.

I realized that once I was triggered, the emotional atmosphere I was living in had become cloudy and inflamed. It became clear to me that my way of reacting in that state of mind would likely not be a wise one. I noticed uneasily that my feelings of compassion, which I had felt for Steven when I first heard of the death of his brother, were starting to decrease. I felt uneasy with myself, with Steven, and with how I would honor my responsibility, not only to the group of students we were teaching, but also to my intention to be true to myself. I decided to go through the steps of compassion, forgiveness, and acceptance for myself. My hope was that my wound with Steven would be healed. I followed the steps that I had written down for my clients and students:

1. Intention Setting

I decided to work through the spiral of compassion meditation by setting an intention so I would have clarity about the process ahead of me and be able to envision how I wanted to feel in the end. My intentions were as follows:

- May I be free of the grudge I am holding in my heart.
- May I have, at the end of the day, a heartfelt relationship with Steven.
- May I be able to align myself with the flow of life-giving energy that runs deeper than our individual stories.
- May I accept whatever will unfold.

Setting such an intention, I knew, was not about controlling the outcome; it would allow me to realign with life and help me ground myself in the flow of life-giving energy. However things would turn out, my intention would be based on that integrity.

2. Mindfully Focusing

I noticed how much I dreaded facilitating the next teaching session with Steven. I took an afternoon off and found a quiet place to be with myself. I went into my backyard with a cushion and found a seat under an apple tree. A short time of Mindfulness Meditation and Loving Awareness Meditation was the best way I knew to calm myself and to center my mind and heart. I sat down comfortably with my back against the bark of the tree, closed my eyes, and decided to just be present with what was coming up for me.

3. Looking Inward

As I meditated under the apple tree, I turned my attention inward with gentleness and warmth. I became aware of all the thoughts, feelings, and images that came up, and I was able to see myself without judgment. Now I could witness what was going on inside myself with understanding and tenderness for what I was experiencing. I realized how confused I was about the right way to go forward. Even though I felt empathy for Steven's family crisis, my experience of hurt was festering. I realized how intensely my painful old patterns had been activated and how much this relationship with Steven reminded me of my family of origin, in which relations had been filled with terse disapproval. Without condoning Steven's behavior, I felt the longing to work through my feelings and free myself from the grudge I was holding.

4. Self-Compassion

Under the apple tree, I was able to feel a new sense of tenderness for the frightened little girl I had once been, who experienced her world as a dark and dangerous place. But I also saw the woman I had become, trying to grow despite these ancient traps. As I reflected on my encounters with Steven, I noticed how afraid I still was of being criticized and rejected. In a meditative state, it was possible to be kind and present with myself. I proceeded to come up with the following phrases of self-compassion:

- May I be able to hold all that is coming up for me gently with kindheartedness and care.
- May I see my own predicament clearly and compassionately.
- May I offer warmth to the little girl I once was, who was so scarred by the circumstances of her early life.
- May I be able to learn and grow toward a new way of being.

5. Self-Forgiveness

When I began to let my walls down and soften a bit, I was able to think more clearly again. Feeling offended by Steven, I had judged myself as too sensitive and weak and had gotten entangled in self-doubt. I recognized how self-centered I had become, as I had been unknowingly protecting my old wounds. At the same time, forgiving myself for my impatience with the highly distressed Steven seemed exceptionally challenging. Through gentle understanding, I was beginning to feel tenderness and caring for myself. Finally I was able to let go of the grudge that I had held toward myself as I repeated these phrases of forgiveness:

- May I let go of the resentment I hold toward myself.
- May I forgive myself for reacting so strongly.
- May I allow myself to start again, new and fresh.
- May I be free.

6. Self-Acceptance

I soon realized that I had to accept myself for exactly who I was at that point in time, including all my remaining foibles and limitations. Such self-acceptance allowed me to feel peace with the reality of the present moment, however imperfect it was. I was able to relax even while knowing that I still felt anxious about my relationship with Steven, that I wanted to hold us both accountable for how we treated each other, and that my grudges could easily rear their ugly heads again.

The following phrases helped me:

- May I accept myself the way I am right now.
- May I love myself even with all my foibles and quirks.
- May I accept my life exactly the way it is.
- May I love my life despite its challenges.
- May self-acceptance accompany me on my path to freedom.

7. Compassion for Others in a Similar Predicament

I still felt tight inside and wondered how the space in my heart could expand most naturally. I extended a feeling of compassion toward those who agonized over similar situation, in this case feelings of rejection or of being judged harshly. In my mind's eye, I envisioned the countless people who battle feelings of insecurity and hurt in their hearts. I thought of my mother, who had felt so rejected by my father, and a friend of mine who had experienced judgment during a painful divorce. I offered caring and warmth toward my mother and my friend, as well as many other people I know:

- May you who are suffering from insecurity and fear be free from suffering.
- May you who are tied up in doubts and self-criticism find freedom and ease.
- May we all be free.

8. Compassion for Steven

I had known before the seminar started that Steven was grieving over the unforeseen loss of his brother. I knew that facilitating a seminar together at this point was risky, but I had not expected it to be as difficult as it was. I strongly felt that Steven did not want to touch the subject of his pain and talk about this experience. Instead, he chose to hold himself rigidly, which contributed to an awful feeling of alienation between us.

It was difficult for me to offer a sense of warmth and caring to Steven. Yet sitting under the apple tree, I quietly spoke the following phrases:

- May you experience healing from the loss you experienced.
- May you hold yourself with gentleness and warmth.
- May I be able to offer you understanding, compassion, and a gentle heart.
- May you be free to love and heal.

9. Forgiveness for Steven

After I sat quietly for a while, I sensed how lost Steven was feeling and that his behavior had most likely been a clumsy way of holding himself together.

I realized that I had to forgive him if I wanted us both to be free. Yet I was carrying around this grudge; I was obsessing about details of our interactions from the past few weeks. Those ruminations were exhausting me.

I struggled with the task of how to forgive while at the same time being authentic and truthful. I returned to the steps I had developed before. Begin with the intention to forgive and allow however long it may take. This is like cracking the door of our hearts open and inviting the gentle winds of grace to breathe through. My wish was to hold an intention of truly feeling compassion and forgiveness, so I came up with the following phrases:

- May I hold the intention to be able, one day, however long it may take, to forgive Steven for ridiculing and censuring me.
- May I hold the wish that one day, however long it may take, Steven and I will be free from criticizing and judging each other.
- May I be able to let go of the grudge toward Steven that I am still carrying around with me.
- May Steven find freedom and happiness in life.
- May we both be free from suffering and the causes of suffering.
- May we both live peacefully and with ease.

Through these steps, I realized that forgiveness is not an all-or-nothing process. Forgiveness does not come at will or all at once. Sometimes it is there and then goes back into hiding. Forgiveness is like a shy deer—we have to give it a lot of space, good will, and patient attention. However, I discovered that compassion, or "walking in the other's moccasins," makes forgiveness more likely.

10. Accepting My Relationship with Steven

Sometimes we can just do as much as we are able to do at a given point in time. With all my efforts toward healing my relationship with Steven, there were still some kernels of dust and dirt that had not been cleaned out. Trust and a sense of warmth had to be reestablished. Only time and revisiting the healing process now and again would lead to true recovery. I began to trust that the time would come when Steven and I could talk about what had happened. Sometimes we have to be gentle and patient with our own process of creating peace with others. The following phrases helped me on this path:

- Just as I am learning to accept myself as I am, may I accept Steven exactly the way he is.
- May I learn to love him with all his quirks and foibles.
- May I accept our relationship exactly the way it is right now.
- May we both live with ease.

11. Well-Wishing for All Beings

As I was feeling lighter and much less burdened, I wanted to send good wishes to all beings everywhere. I prayed,

- May all beings be well.
- May all beings live with peace.

I included in my well-wishing all those close by, those far away, those I knew, those I did not know, those I liked, those I had a hard time caring about, those who were hungry, those who were well fed, those living in times of peace, those living in times of war.

I wanted to offer acceptance and love for the world exactly as it is right now. I included humans, animals and creatures, trees, rocks, plants, the land, the waters, the skies, beings now, beings who had been alive in the past, and beings who will be living long after we are gone in future times.

12. Gratitude

Offering compassion, forgiveness, and acceptance felt challenging, but it also brought a surprising sense of relief. I felt raw in my heart. I was grateful that I had the tools to let go of the heavy burden of resentment and that I was able to come to a place of acceptance of what is. In my mind, I said,

- May I be grateful to be able to work through this difficult entanglement with Steven.
- May I be thankful for this chance to be free (or to free myself).

I experienced my heart as wide and open, and felt the longing to share this feeling with others. I prayed,

- May the benefits of this meditation go out into the world and beyond.

I imagined the dark rain clouds that had been hanging over Steven's and my fateful relationship giving way to a clear blue sky.

As I worked with the spiral of compassion meditation, I gradually became able to reengage in the rest of Steven's and my work together. The last days of our seminar were surprisingly pleasant and much more relaxed. A few months after the seminar was over, Steven and I had lunch together. With the passing of time, he was now able to talk about what had happened and how shocked and frightened he had been during his family crisis. We were even able to address his awkward and even hurtful behavior toward me. By the time we reached coffee and a chocolate tart, we had decided that the most important thing was to be friends again.

Key Points

- Together, mindfulness, compassion, and forgiveness give you a chance to revisit and possibly heal hurt relationships.
- Even if you may not be able to heal the injured relationship, you can find resolution and freedom for yourself.
- Feeling compassion and forgiveness for yourself may make it possible to feel compassion and forgiveness for others.

- Letting go of a grudge toward yourself and/or others allows you to recover valuable life energy that may have been used to keep your resentment in check.
- Letting go of an old grudge allows you to move forward and establish new, unburdened relationships.

JOURNAL EXERCISE

Sit down with a pencil and paper in a quiet place. Make yourself comfortable, rest in your gentle breath, and see what images and stories arise as you read the following prompts. If your own experiences come to mind, do some free writing.

1. Describe a time when you felt hurt or angered by someone and found it difficult to offer forgiveness.
2. Imagine offering forgiveness now—to yourself and to the other person(s). Describe how that happened and what it felt like.
3. If you were not able to access a feeling of forgiveness, imagine going through the twelve steps of this practice and do some free writing about what comes up.

15

Brief On-the-Go Practices for Mindfulness and Compassion

With the brief Mindfulness On-the-Go practices, you can find a specific practice that is most relevant to a challenge you face in your life. These practices are portable. You can carry a card in your wallet that includes a practice relevant to your situation. Please find on-the-go cards as adjunct to practices in the book. You can also fill the Compassionate Choice Practice Worksheet in on the website Mindfulpause.org. Challenges you face may include difficult moods like sadness, anger, and fear, or a life situation such as illness, conflict, loss, or uncertainty.

A brief mindful pause practice can help you bring mindfulness and compassion right into the moment during an everyday challenge. Even when you have only a few minutes to spare, you can choose a practice to offer you a few practical steps to find your balance again. Brief practices can support deep work and complement some of the other longer practices.

The Mindfulness On-the-Go practices do not cover every difficulty, but the diversity of the examples in this chapter will show you the potential for bringing mindfulness and compassion into any challenging situation you may confront. Working with these practices in the here and now will eventually teach you to create a practice for yourself when you encounter a stressful situation.

One of the most important themes in Buddhist practice is awareness, meaning to be "awake and present" to what is going on. Often thoughts and actions cloud what is really happening and trap you in a ball of pain. By looking at yourself skillfully, you can gently free knots of hurt and confusion. Mindfulness On-the-Go practices are especially useful in bringing awareness into all the nooks and crannies of your daily life.

Each brief practice includes a sequence of phrases that are easy to follow. As you become aware that something upsetting has happened, you notice the sensations and emotions that follow. Awareness helps you slow down the reactive process. The experience of your body's felt sense is crucial for doing these practices, especially when difficult emotions arise. Compassion for your own experience allows you to feel understood and for your heart to calm down. The flow of breath allows you to experience yourself as part of the bigger flow of life. Then you can see clearly and with a wiser perspective what may be your next step forward.

The following exercise presents the most universal version of a Mindfulness On-the-Go practice:

⟜ WHEN I FEEL TRIGGERED

1. I notice my body.
2. I choose to pause.
3. I exhale gently to relax.
4. I recognize my feelings.
5. I sense my heart.
6. I offer compassion to myself.
7. When I am ready, I reengage.

MINDFULNESS ON-THE-GO PRACTICES FOR VARIOUS MOODS AND PREDICAMENTS

The practices that follow have the same general structure but with specific instructions tailored for different situations. In fact, all of the Mindfulness On-the-Go practices follow the principle of the brief mindful pause. There are many reasons why you may be triggered and lose your inner balance. A brief and relevant practice of mindfulness and compassion will help you to find your way through those difficult situations to a place of participating with loving awareness in your life.

When I Feel Stressed

Last year, my daughter Bella felt particularly stressed in college. Chemistry seemed too hard for this slight, twenty-year-old blond with inquisitive dark brown eyes. She began to have trouble sleeping and complained of stomachaches as well as thinning hair. Needless to say, Bella was thrown off balance. When we were sitting together over a mom-and-daughter dinner, I was surprised that Bella asked me to create a short Mindfulness On-the-Go practice for her. She hoped that she could practice the phrases between classes or before studying in the library. I sent her a card with the following exercise:

⌒ WHEN I FEEL STRESSED

1. I notice where I feel stress in my body.
2. I choose to press a metaphorical blue pause button.
3. I exhale gently to relax.
4. I recognize that I am hurting and that I have lost my balance.
5. I feel the tender breath of my heart.
6. I hold my predicament with kindness and offer compassion to myself.

7. I return to the breath as a refuge and notice when I am ready to reengage with my life.

Bella began to integrate this practice into her day. The brief practice gave her the relaxation response and resilience needed to pull through her chemistry class. Noticing the sequence of feelings in her body allowed her to recognize how much discomfort she was in and to respond with kindness rather than self-criticism. This was new and helpful to her. I was happy and surprised when Bella told me a few weeks later that her roommate Kaya had found the piece of paper with the Mindfulness On-the-Go practice. Kaya had pinned it on the communal refrigerator for all the roommates facing final exams. Loving awareness and compassion had become an essential part of Bella's education.

When I Want to Shut Down

Recently Dana, a young woman in her late twenties, came to my office. While she was already a passionate meditator, she had been struggling for a few years with a variety of physical problems that caused her increasing stress. Fibromyalgia and other autoimmune-related symptoms had left her riddled with body pain and exhaustion.

Despite her usually bright affect and the support of her doctors, Dana felt more and more discouraged and dejected. In addition to her physical problems, she was also an exquisitely sensitive person who became easily overwhelmed by strong stimuli and life's demands. One day when she felt particularly overcome, she asked me to design a Mindfulness On-the-Go practice for her that she could use when she felt the strong urge to contract into herself.

Together we designed a practice that fit her internal experience. Dana hoped that such a practice would support her meditation practice, ground her in the present moment, help her relax, and allow her to remain open to others. She also wanted it to help her to regain a sense of hope and connectedness so she could be more present in her life again.

We came up with the following phrases:

⌐ WHEN I FEEL LIKE SHUTTING DOWN

1. I notice the sensations in my body.
2. I choose to pause so that something new can happen.
3. I exhale gently to relax.
4. I recognize my urge to retreat, contract, and isolate myself.
5. I feel the breath of my heart.
6. I am gentle with my feelings and offer compassion to myself.
7. I take refuge in the sensations and movements of breath, and let go all the way until my breath connects me with the web of life.

Focusing on her body through this practice ultimately helped Dana to be present in her life again and to disengage from her strong urge to turn inward. As she attended to the sensations of her out-breath, something in her began to open. The big breath of the world worked as a poetic metaphor for her experience, allowing her to reconnect to an always changing, expansive sense of reality. She experienced a feeling of inter-connectedness as she allowed her breath to join the "big breath." This allowed her feelings of loneliness and separation to dissolve naturally, as she felt connected to something bigger than herself.

When I Am in a Bad Mood

The following On-the-Go example was created with my daughter Bella and two of her girlfriends. On a summer Saturday, I had planned to go to the print shop on the way into town to pick up a box of Mindfulness On-the-Go cards for my clients. After I had picked them up, I wanted to treat Bella and her friends to a visit to the nail salon. I was curious to see how the three girls would take to the little cards. To my surprise, they all loved them. Kaya said, "I wish there was a card for when I'm in a bad mood." Bella agreed that that would be very helpful, especially when dealing with her difficult roommate. Kaya added, "I know that we can turn things around when we want to." Then she looked at me quizzically and added, "But how?"

Sitting in our reclining chairs, enjoying the pampering of having our nails done, we worked together on the practice. The Vietnamese student employee at the salon and several other female customers joined the discussion. Together we tried to find the right wording for a "when I am in a bad mood" practice. After some conversation, we decided on the following phrases:

⌒ WHEN I AM IN A BAD MOOD

1. I notice what is going on in my body.
2. I choose to press the pause button and allow for change.
3. I recognize the emotions that keep me entangled.
4. I take refuge in the sensations and movements of breath and allow breath to breathe me.
5. Without grasping or pushing away, I allow my difficult thoughts, feelings, and moods to pass by like clouds in the sky.
6. I know that all is change and ultimately okay.

In Kaya's opinion, the most important aspect of practice was learning to let go of problematic thoughts and resist the seduction to stay stuck in them. She noted, "We have to surrender our big egos to the flow of breath." To get there, she recommended that the wording be upbeat and direct. She suggested the phrase "Choose and allow for a change." Kikka, an Italian girl with dark, unruly curls and bright, laughing eyes, liked the idea of thoughts passing by like clouds in the sky. Kaya introduced the idea of focusing on what was going well in your life. She had learned that way of looking at life from her dad, a chiropractor. All of them voted for the phrase "Know that all is change and ultimately okay."

My experience with the girls was an excellent example of cocreating a Mindfulness On-the-Go practice based on what was needed in the moment. Together we found a way to make this practice relevant and accessible to those who need it.

When I Feel Sad

Kim, an eighteen-year-old high school senior, was sad. Her girlfriend was going off to a university in another state, but Kim had to stay in town to attend the local community college. Her family did not have the money to send her away to school.

Kim's mother had just had a double mastectomy as part of cancer treatment, and Kim was expected to help out at home. Usually she was a sparkly young woman with plenty of friends, but now she felt discouraged. Being gay in this little town and alone without her girlfriend's love made her feel especially vulnerable. She knew that there was not much she could do besides performing the chores her family expected and making the best of a difficult situation.

Often Kim took her sheepdog, Skippy, and went for long walks on the beach. She loved having her headphones on and listening to music. She enjoyed the glimmer of bright colors on the ocean, especially in the early morning, and the beautiful pink skies in the early evening. During a family counseling session, I gave Kim one of my cards with short phrases. One day, when Kim took her walk, she sat down on the beach and took out her card for When I Feel Sad and followed the steps:

⟿ WHEN I FEEL SAD

1. I notice the feelings of sadness in my body.
2. I sense the breath of my heart.
3. I turn to myself with gentleness and care.
4. I feel the breath of life brushing through the contracted, heavy undergrowth that weighs down my heart.

5. I allow myself to accept exactly where I am right now.
6. When I am ready, I begin to listen to the sounds and colors connecting me to a bigger field.
7. If there is a spark of joy, I welcome it back.

A few weeks later, I saw Kim again. She laughed and said, "I liked your card." Then she went on to tell me about what happened when she did the practice on the card. "At first," she said, "I felt so sad and alone, stuck here in this town. My heart felt so heavy and dense. I missed Paula, my girlfriend, a lot." After a pause, she continued, "As I allowed myself to feel the hurting strain, I was more able to be okay with what is going on right now. The phrase, 'Feel the breath of life brushing through the contracted, heavy undergrowth that weighs down my heart' described my feelings accurately. Something inside of me felt understood."

She added, "Then suddenly I felt a lot lighter. The contraction in my chest let go. I realized that no matter what, I love life." The brief When I Feel Sad practice had helped Kim to leave her isolated and disillusioned state of heart and mind and to find a way to be open to love again.

When There Is Tension and Hurt between Couples and Pairs

Santiago and Ashley met in one of my meditation groups six years ago. Two years later, they got married. Now they were in my office, each sitting turned away from each other in their respective chairs. The atmosphere seemed tense. Santiago, an energetic Mexican-American man with dark and silver curls, worked as a surgeon at the local hospital. Ashley, a designer from an Anglo family, had been brought up in a well-to-do area of San Francisco, while Santiago had had to be tough as he worked his way out of the projects of East Los Angeles.

The night before our session, the two of them had become ensnared in an agonizing struggle. It had been a Friday evening, and Santiago was particularly exhausted. Ashley said that he had been insensitive and even rude to her when she wanted to tell him about a concert she was looking forward to attending. Santiago felt that Ashley had put him "into a box" as "rough and uneducated" and not valuing culture. The argument quickly escalated. Santiago had stormed out and retreated into the guest bedroom for the night.

The couple started arguing with each other in my office, trying to defend their respective positions. I gently requested their attention and asked them if they were willing to try an experiment with a brief practice.

⊸ WHEN THERE IS TENSION AND HURT BETWEEN COUPLES AND PAIRS

1. Notice the sensations in your bodies.
2. Choose to press the metaphorical pause button.
3. Notice the energy of distress in the room.
4. Exhale gently to relax.
5. Sense the breath of your heart.
6. Feel your suffering and offer compassion to yourself.
7. Allow yourself to open to each other's energy.
8. Realize that both of you want to be happy most of all.
9. Imagine walking in each other's shoes for a little while.
10. If you are able, allow for the possibility of taking the other person's point of view and feeling his or her hurt.
11. Keep returning to the breath as a refuge.
12. When you are ready, meet each other with openness and respect.

When the guided practice had ended, Santiago and Ashley looked more relaxed. I asked what had come up during the practice. Ashley quietly relayed that she was now able to recognize how tired Santiago had been on Friday evening. She also shared a memory from when she was eight years old: her father had left the house in a fury, and Ashley had felt scared and abandoned.

Santiago shared memories of a rigid Anglo teacher he'd had in fourth grade; she had criticized and punished him for being a loud and raucous

Mexican. He also remembered how painful it had been to be the "Mexican" at the Ivy League medical school where he had trained.

After they had shared their feelings and memories, both seemed softer as they glanced at each other. They asked for cards to take home. They were more relaxed for the time being, able to see each other with more compassionate eyes. Understanding leads to compassion. Mindfulness and compassion together allowed them to slow down and become quiet enough to hear each other's experience. The Mindfulness On-the-Go practice was helpful here as part of Santiago and Ashley's continuing work to integrate their differences.

⟿ WHEN TRAUMA HAS LEFT YOU GRIEVING WHAT HAS BEEN LOST

(Recommended for PTSD)

Last year I was introduced to Dr. Leishram, a clinical psychologist visiting our local university from Nepal. He had worked in a Nepalese camp with refugees from Bhutan. Many of the exiles had experienced trauma and loss. "How can mindfulness and compassion practice help those I work with?" Dr. Leishram asked. "What practices can I teach to those who are so traumatized?"

After talking with Dr. Leishram for a while, I understood that the symptoms of those at the camp included anxiety, grief, and anger. Dr. Leishram assured me that he could easily translate my Mindfulness On-the-Go practices and make them culturally relevant for the refugees he worked with. As many of them suffered from the aftereffects of sickness, hunger, and the death of family members, as well as an undercurrent of constant anxiety, this was the first practice I recommended:

⟿ WHEN I FEEL SCARED

1. I notice the sensations in my body.
2. I feel the gentle flow of my out-breath.
3. I recognize feelings of anxiety and numbness.

4. I allow myself to lean into the felt sense of my feelings.
5. I offer understanding and compassion for myself and my journey.
6. I sense the breath of my heart connecting me to the flow of life.
7. I recognize when I am ready to reengage with others.

As many of the refugees had experienced great loss, I added the following phrases:

⌖ WHEN I FEEL GRIEF FOR A LOSS

1. I notice the feelings in my heart.
2. I gently follow my out-breath to relax.
3. I recognize feelings of sadness, grief, and even hopelessness.
4. I gently lean into the felt sense of that experience, getting comfort from the warmth of my out-breath.
5. I offer compassion and care to myself and accept my life's journey as it is right now.
6. Attention and breath flow together, allowing breath to breathe me.
7. For a moment I experience myself as part of life.

Often those who have lost their home and country don't know how to work with their anger and frustration about what they have lost and the life they are no longer able to live. It is necessary to find the middle path of feeling and sensing deeply yet not acting out in destructive ways.

Although many of us have not had to face such an extreme situation, each of us can relate to how anger and frustration feel when our life circumstances are challenging. This can cause us to behave destructively to both others and ourselves. Feelings of powerlessness and shame can cause additional misery. A relevant mindful pause practice can give us a kind of "psychospiritual container" and the support we need to find our balance again and act in wise and compassionate ways.

⟿ WHEN I AM ANGRY

1. I notice the sensations of contraction and tightness in my body.
2. I choose to press the metaphorical pause button and decide to try something new.
3. I reconnect to my yearning to find peace of mind and heart.
4. I recognize my feelings of rage, anger, resentment, and frustration.
5. I lightly lean into the felt sense of those emotions.
6. With compassion and understanding, I gently contain the ferocity of my feelings.
7. I surrender to the flow of breath connecting me to a much broader perspective.

At times it may be helpful to add a few more phrases that help you join a bigger perspective beyond your own predicament. Your fear, grief, or resentment can make you preoccupied with yourself. Even though something in you has the urge to turn your attention exclusively toward your own worries, it can be healing for you to expand your awareness to a broader point of view. After point 7 in the preceding list, you might add the following phrases:

1. In my mind's eye, I remember those many others who have experienced trauma and loss and also suffer from feelings of rage, grief, and fear.
2. I expand my compassion and well-wishing to all those and their families and say, "May we all be well, may we all be safe, may we all receive the support we need to heal and grow."
3. Surrendering to the flow of breath, the flow of life, connects all of us to a wider and kinder perspective.

With the tenderness and persistence of these brief Mindfulness On-the-Go practices complementing the longer mindfulness and compassion practices, your painful feelings and long-held suffering can gradually soften and transform into wisdom and an increased ability to tend to the suffering of others.

FURTHER MINDFULNESS ON-THE-GO PRACTICES

The following practices can help you bring mindfulness and compassion to a variety of challenging situations in your life. See if some fit your experience and seem helpful to you.

↶ WHEN SOMEONE YELLS AT ME

1. I notice the signs of stress in my body.
2. I recognize that I am scared, numb, or upset.
3. I feel the support of the ground under my feet.
4. I exhale gently to relax.
5. I offer compassion to myself for what I experienced.
6. I recognize that I don't have to take it personally.
7. I take refuge in my breath until I feel in balance again.

↶ WHEN I FEEL CRITICIZED OR SNUBBED

1. I notice the sensations in my body.
2. I recognize my feelings (frustration, hurt, anger, shame).
3. I feel the support of the ground under my feet and realize that I am part of a bigger field.
4. I exhale gently to relax.
5. I stay with my feelings and offer compassion to myself.
6. I notice the conflicted energy of the other is coming at me yet stay grounded within my own heart.
7. I take a breath and breathe quietly until I feel my balance again.

⤙ WHEN I FEEL WOUNDED OR ALONE

1. I notice these feelings in my body.
2. I choose to pause.
3. I gently follow the sensations of my out-breath.
4. With gentle kindness, I hold my experience of being hurt and broken.
5. I extend compassion to myself.
6. I feel the breath of my heart.
7. I allow for the possibility that I am part of a mutually coarising intelligent field.
8. I know that I can bring that unbroken wisdom and benevolence into my life.

⤙ WHEN I FEEL AFRAID

1. I notice my body's feelings with kindness.
2. I exhale gently to relax.
3. I recognize the little child in my heart who feels shaky and scared.
4. I feel the breath of my heart.
5. Accepting my experience, I offer compassion to myself.
6. Joining the flow, I allow my body to be breathed.
7. I notice when I am ready to reengage.

⤙ WHEN I DREAD CONTACT WITH ANOTHER

1. I notice the sensations in my body.
2. I exhale gently to relax.
3. I recognize my aversion to engaging with the other person.
4. I sense the breath of my heart.
5. I pause to offer compassion to myself and hold my own trepidation with kindness.

6. I hold my reluctance with gentle understanding.
7. I recognize that the other person and I both ultimately want to be happy and allow for the possibility of meeting one another with peace and respect.
8. I return to the breath as refuge, and notice when I feel ready to connect.

⌐◦ WHEN I FEEL OVERWHELMED BY ANOTHER'S PAIN

1. I notice the sensations in my body.
2. I exhale gently to relax.
3. I feel my pain about the other's suffering.
4. I sense the breath of my heart.
5. I offer compassion to myself.
6. I return to breath as interconnecting flow.
7. When I am ready, I meet the other in pain.

⌐◦ WHEN I HAVE LOST MY BALANCE

1. I notice what the imbalance feels like in my body.
2. I recognize the pull of my emotions to fix this painful situation.
3. I gently follow the sensation and movement of my breath, allowing my body to be breathed.
4. I feel my body relaxing with each out-breath and continue to let go beyond the out-breath.
5. I allow myself to be held by the intelligence of the field around me.
6. While offering compassion to myself, I accept what is.
7. I slowly look around the room and am ready to be here right now.

These practices have helped me to work gently with my discomfort, fear, and irritation when I have needed to face difficult times. I hope they and other practices will allow you to bring more awareness, kindness, compassion, and ultimately happiness into the cobwebbed corners of your daily life. I hope also that when you are in need, you will be inspired to create Mindfulness On-the-Go practices of your own.

- May we all find happiness.
- Maybe we all feel understood and recognized for who we are.
- May we all be able to give and receive love.
- May our understanding for ourselves lead to compassion and care for others.

Key Points

- Mindfulness On-the-Go practices allow you to bring mindfulness and compassion to your daily life challenges.
- During both peaceful and unsettled times, these practices become more beautiful with increased awareness and compassion.
- Besides formal meditation practice, you need to develop relevant and accessible ways of bringing mindfulness and compassion into more times of imbalance and upset.
- On-the-go practices give you brief phrases, or creative mantras, that can be relevant to the difficult situations you encounter during your daily life.
- These brief practices teach self-awareness, self-compassion, connecting to breath and heart, and lead you to hold a wider perspective.
- These practices can be customized to fit your specific circumstances.
- When you feel understood and accurately seen, when you are able to stop judging yourself, and when you lean into the deep felt sense of your experience, then your heart can open to love and life.

JOURNAL EXERCISE

Sit down with a pencil and paper in a quiet place. Make yourself comfortable, rest in your gentle breath, and see what images and stories arise as you read the following prompts. If your own experiences come to mind, do some free writing.

1. Think of times in your daily life when you are easily thrown out of balance and wish you could feel more mindful, compassionate, and at peace. Do some free writing.
2. Take one of those times and describe the atmosphere, time of day, people present, and what happened. Now choose one of the On-the-Go practices and imagine going through the proposed steps. Describe your experience.
3. Take another incident where you were thrown out of balance. Create an image of what happened in your mind's eye and sense the atmosphere in your body. Now create phrases that fit the feeling tone of your experience and help you find your balance again.

Stories

16

Introducing Nine Stories

Part Three of this book presents stories of people like you and me who struggle with common predicaments. These people may have money problems, suffer from self-loathing, or feel betrayed or angry. We all have been hurt, and we may have—knowingly or unknowingly—inflicted harm. This is an inevitable aspect of our shared humanity. Although we often cannot prevent such misfortunes from happening, we can learn to become aware of our thoughts, feelings, desires, and aversions. It is from knowing and understanding that we can help ourselves to stop the cycles of hurt, fear, depression, or anger to which we are all vulnerable in one way or another.

The practices introduced in Part Two have given you tools to be increasingly present with compassionate awareness. The mindfulness practices have given you the foundation to focus inward, to see your experiences more clearly, and to cultivate your wisdom mind. The compassion practices have given you ways to recognize and heal your own wounds so you can include both yourself and others on your path.

The upcoming stories show how you can prevent your reactivity from destroying your relationships and how, with the help of a mindful pause and steadily refined reflection, to create an increasingly well-balanced life. I hope these stories will both dramatize the complexity with which life unfolds and offer examples of various practices you can use to navigate that complexity with kindness and equanimity.

As you recognize yourself and people familiar to you in these stories, and as you follow how the people in the stories find their way to more freedom and happiness, it will become more apparent to you how you can disentangle complications in your own life. I will show how the practices described in Part Two can complement each other to offer people in distress ways to find more health, happiness, and freedom as they face their all-too-human challenges.

Journal questions once more allow you to explore the depth of your own experience and to bring compassionate understanding to your inner life. These invitations to reflect and write also help you to imagine ways to develop your practice. Paving an "imaginary pathway" in your journal may make it easier for you to implement changes in your practice life and in your relationships. Then you can dedicate the fruits of your practice to the curvy path you wander—and to your world.

17

When You Experience Self-Criticism

This is a story about Max, a high school teacher who experienced a great deal of self-criticism. With the help of Mindfulness Meditation, Loving Awareness Meditation, the Self-Compassion Practice, and Mindfulness On-the-Go practices, he was able to transform old habits of self-loathing and make friends with himself.

Max, a well-liked high school teacher, was in a high state of anxiety and distress. When I went to greet him on a late Monday afternoon, the short, wiry man was pacing up and down the wooden veranda outside my office. As he burst into the consultation room, he moved his fingers fervently through his enormous head of sandy-colored curls. He announced that he had lived through an extraordinarily upsetting weekend.

Everything started when he woke up on Sunday morning from a troubling dream, one that was full of panic about his work. He felt haunted by images of several of his students who had gotten into trouble with drugs and been picked up by the police.

However, the anxiety and agitation had started after his father's death one year earlier and now had trickled into Max's work at school. A few times he had gotten into arguments with two of his male colleagues. Complaints had been taken to the school board. The principal, an older woman who cared about Max, suggested that he come to see me for therapy. During the next two years of working together, we revisited Max's relationship with his father, which had been complicated and left Max feeling guilty and uneasy. Together we tried to understand how the patterns left over from that difficult relationship were still affecting Max's current life. His father had often criticized Max. Even when the older man was dying, he had pushed Max away, not allowing his son to become close and at peace with him.

The day before I found him on my veranda, Max had gotten out of bed on the wrong side of what should have been a good Sunday morning and a day off work. Trying to be gracious to his wife, he agreed to a beach walk with their three dogs. However, even on the car ride to the beach, he could not let go of his tension. Then things went from bad to worse. While driving, he burned his lip on the coffee cup. And when the dogs started to bark and fight in the car, he lost it. Max threw his cup full of hot coffee at the dogs, yelling at them and his wife. He ended up kicking his yellow lab, Samson, whom he blamed as the troublemaker.

For an hour he stomped along the beach without saying a word, frustrated with himself. He was not enjoying the day. While walking back, he berated his wife with a tirade of harsh words. After they returned home, Max retreated into his office to do paperwork. He wanted to hide away from everybody. He told me later that this was when he started to feel extremely depressed and low. He felt hatred for himself and remorse and disgust for his actions. A barrage of self-criticism followed the onslaught of blame he had flung at those around him.

At our session, Max told me how much self-loathing he still felt about those events, even a day later. In addition to being his therapist, I was also Max's meditation teacher. During meditation practice, he had at times experienced a ground of goodness and peace beneath his mundane, troubled surface. Yet in times of stress, it was close to impossible for Max to stay connected with this experience and insight. He was suffering from his own reactivity, and it was difficult for him to allow for a break in his self-criticism. Therefore I encouraged him to take a pause with one of the Mindfulness On-the-Go practices when destructive and self-loathing impulses came up in response to upsetting experiences. Together we devised a practice that promised to fit his predicament:

⤚ WHEN I FEEL CRITICAL OF MYSELF

1. I notice the signs of tension and stress in my body.
2. I recognize the felt sense of self-loathing as it manifests itself in my body.
3. I kindly choose to press the pause button.
4. I feel breath brushing through the area of my heart and notice how my heart is responding to self-criticism.
5. Without judgment, I feel my feelings and offer compassion to myself.
6. I remember that at my core, the basis of my being is goodness and peace.
7. I join the flow of breath, and allow breath to breathe me.

During this visit, Max was able to examine his underlying triggers. He realized how stressed he had felt recently. He recognized how overwhelming the bureaucracy and the magnitude of his steadily increasing workload had been and how worried he was about some of his students. Several students had recently failed academically while battling severe family problems. A few more had resorted to drugs as distraction and escape from what they could not face in their lives.

In the safety of my office, Max allowed himself to realize how helpless he felt in trying to make things better for the kids in his care. He came to see that he lived within a huge field of reactivity and upset, an atmosphere in which the people around him were overwhelmed, irritated, and burned out. I realized how traumatized Max had become by the challenges at school. There were too few resources and staff to address the problems effectively. This situation had left him numb and too exhausted to care about his own life. It helped Max to hear that his reaction to stress at school was common, maybe even normal. He reminded himself to try to stop taking upsets at school so personally, and he started to seem a bit more relaxed.

As he was sitting in the brown leather chair, the tension he had been holding in his body decreased. He let out a big breath and allowed his head to rest on the back of the chair. His tight jaw muscles seemed to drop an inch. Understanding the connection between his stress, self-reproach, and reactivity allowed Max to accept that he needed to take better care of himself. Before he left the session, we made a plan. He would rejoin the gym, go out sailing with one of his buddies, and revisit a men's group. As part of his ongoing care program, Max decided to allow more time for cultivating mindfulness. He decided to practice a half hour in the morning and a half hour in the afternoon when he came home from work. Once a week he would go to his meditation group. Mindfulness and compassion practice gave Max a supportive and nourishing container, allowing him to see himself clearly and with kind attention.

One afternoon, when he relaxed in the chair in my office, Max also made the connection to childhood events. Doing so finally allowed him to feel compassion for himself and recognize that he had learned a habit of flaring up with anger from his father. As he remembered his childhood, he recognized a pattern of deep-seated self-hatred in his father as well as in himself. I recommended a specific practice of self-compassion as an antidote to the self-hatred he was so used to. At first Max was resistant to that suggestion. Growing up, he had learned the habit of faulting himself and believed in the notion that self-blame and even self-condemnation could be redemptive and even purifying. Yet he began to realize that this strategy did not work anymore. After some reluctance, he agreed to repeat the following phrases to himself:

- May I hold myself with gentleness.
- May I be free from self-criticism and condemnation.
- May I extend compassion toward this bruised heart of mine.

- May I extend understanding and warmth toward myself as I experience the feelings of upset and anger.
- May I extend compassion toward myself as I attempt to soften these old feelings of self-loathing and alienation.
- May I be free from suffering and the causes of suffering.
- May I find the support I need to become balanced again.

After he recited these phrases, Max spontaneously felt warmth toward those who had been trapped with him in the disastrous Sunday morning encounter. Thinking of his wife and dogs, he whispered,

- May you be free.
- May you be free and safe and well.
- May you be free from suffering and the causes of suffering.
- May you find the support you need.
- May life rise up to meet you.

Old grudges hold a person tethered and burdened. Those who hurt you may have long since disappeared from your life, yet you may still squander your precious energy with feelings of disdain, remorse, or even hate.

After he sent kind thoughts to his wife and dogs, Max murmured to his father,

- May you be free, wherever you are now.
- May I be able to extend understanding and care toward you and your predicament.
- May I be able to forgive you.
- May I be able to forgive myself.
- May I be able to set you free in the spirit of wisdom and compassion.

At first, this new way of expressing kindheartedness and compassion to himself seemed strange and unfamiliar to Max and difficult to integrate into his daily life. He was a strong man who liked to work out and sail. So much vulnerability felt awkward to him. After a while, however, as he repeated the self-compassion phrases over and over again, he started to feel relief. Furthermore, he noticed how his heart, even though it was still smarting, felt tenderer. Over the following weeks, he began to be able to tolerate images of himself as a little boy crouching under a table while being scared by his father's outbursts. Then images of himself on that awful Sunday morning came up—so hurting, so beside himself, so lost. Now he felt kindness toward himself. After he sent self-compassion to himself, images of his wife, the dogs, and his own children and pupils rose to the surface of his consciousness, and he viewed them with tenderness.

Often as you open up your heart, feelings of kindness, compassion, forgiveness, and generosity well up naturally and flow outward in widening circles. For Max, images of his work, the difficulties with the bureaucracy, the fiscal crisis in the educational system, and the faces of his young students and fellow teachers surfaced. In a meeting about six weeks after his tantrum on the beach, Max told me how much compassion he felt for all those entangled in the difficult task of educating the young in a school system that was understaffed and underpaid. Together, we thought of phrases that would seem accessible him and relevant to his situation. Then Max prayed quietly,

- May I extend compassion toward myself in this painful, often discouraging work environment.
- May I have the courage to continue on my path of teaching while holding myself gently and patiently.
- May I also give gratitude for the inspiring moments I share with my students.
- May I be grateful for my colleagues, who bravely accompany me on this trying journey.
- May I extend my care and warmth and well-wishing to all children in this world and to their parents, as we struggle along to be safe, to have food and shelter, and to learn.
- May we all receive the support we need so we can grow and be happy and free.

Max's heart felt raw now. However, in that seeming vulnerability, he felt stronger, kinder, and surprisingly safe.

Max's story demonstrates how your habit of self-deprecation and self-reproach can be healed by daring to look inward and holding your inner experience with understanding, gentleness, and care. The self-criticism you experience often originates from trauma, from having being treated harshly, or from feeling deficient and burned out by your life's tasks. By working with Mindfulness Meditation, Loving Awareness Meditation, and the Self-Compassion Practice, as well as Mindfulness On-the-Go practices, you can face your old deep wounds and hurts, as well as those you have caused other people. The Self-Compassion Practice creates the safe container for true work on yourself and prepares the road for your transformation, so you and those around you can become happier, more alive, and free.

RELATED PRACTICES

When I Feel Critical of Myself—Chapter 17, page 147
The Self-Compassion Practice—Chapter 10, page 68
The Compassion for Others Practice—Chapter 11, pages 78–79

JOURNAL EXERCISE

Sit down with a pencil and paper in a quiet place. Make yourself comfortable, rest in your gentle breath, and see what images and stories arise as you read the following prompts. If your own experiences come to mind, do some free writing.

1. List a few times when you have been harsh or disapproving with yourself.
2. Select one of those times and describe where you were, what prompted your self-criticism, and how it felt in your body.
3. Select one of the on-the-go self-compassion practices and imagine yourself practicing with phrases relevant to your situation. Envision how the situation could have taken a different turn.

18

When Old Family Wounds Haunt You

Heidi faced and healed the trauma that had been passed down for generations in her family. Making peace with herself through compassion and bodhichitta practices, as well as with daily Loving Awareness Meditation, helped her confront her own difficult feelings and learn from the problematic events that had been triggered by past wounds.

Heidi was a Mexican woman in her midfifties with a lively face and passionate feelings. In our therapy sessions, she talked to me about her work as a family therapist for mothers and children who had experienced trauma. One day she unexpectedly turned to me and asked, "Can I talk to you about something?" She continued with urgency, "There are these little mute kids coming into the clinic, little Mexican children. They are so very shy, and they don't say anything. I ask them questions, comment on their pretty dresses, but they stay completely silent."

I responded, "That is sad for you and them."

Heidi shook her black curls vigorously, looked at me with a fierce gaze, and responded, "I get so angry at them; those kids completely frustrate me." She paused, then asked quietly, "Radhule, why do I get so mad at them? I am terrible!"

When I asked her if she had feelings and memories that reminded her of those wordless children, Heidi became quiet. After a while, she replied, "My mom and dad came from Mexico City to the United States when I was a year old. We were dirt poor. First we lived in Texas, then, after a few years, we came to Los Angeles. By then I had several younger sisters. I remember a time when my mother sent me out to go to a store. I was supposed to ask for certain items we needed. You know, as a five-year-old, I spoke better English than she did. But I was frightened to go and talk to these people. I became completely numb and mute, frozen. At those times, my mother got very angry and hissed at me, '*No seas Indio.* Don't be an Indian.'"

Heidi let her head drop and stayed silent for a while. "Indians were the lowest class of people in Mexican society. What a terrible thing to say to me and about Indios." Then she continued, "But why do I become so mad at those poor little kids?" Heidi looked at me with a puzzled and tormented expression.

I explained that, unknowingly, we often repeat our parents' behavior, which originates from unconscious habits. I added that we all do this, and we do not need to judge ourselves for acting that way.

"What can I do?" Heidi looked at me with pleading eyes.

I suggested that she bring her attention to the feelings in her body. After following her breath for a while, Heidi looked more grounded and present. Like Ariadne's thread, breath and awareness connected her deep inner experience to the present moment. I knew that Heidi liked working with mindfulness and compassion meditations. Therefore I recommended that she engage in a Self-Compassion Practice, which might help to bring an attitude of understanding and self-acceptance to what was going on inside. I suggested that she also include those silent little children in her compassion prayer. Together we created a number of phrases that seemed to fit Heidi's experience:

- May I hold my feelings of anger and frustration toward those
  mute children with understanding and gentleness.
- May I be patient with myself as I become aware of what is going
  on inside myself.
- May I offer feelings of warmth and compassion to myself, even
  when it is hard to tolerate my reactivity.
- May I look at myself without judgment and with a caring heart.
- May I include the little frightened girl I once was in my caring.
- May she and I be free.

Heidi pushed her bouncy curls behind her ears and smiled. "That feels better; my heart was tied in a knot."

I asked, "Could we expand those phrases to include compassion for those frightened kids that are landing in your office?" We thought of phrases together that would hit the sweet spot of representing accurately what Heidi was feeling.

After a moment of breathing quietly, Heidi continued her prayer:

- May I include those frightened children I meet every day in my
  loving care.
- May they receive the support they need to find their new home
  in this country.
- May they and their parents receive the encouragement and
  compassion essential to finding happiness and ease.

When I saw Heidi two weeks later, she told me that the compassion practice had helped her immensely. She reported that she now took a few minutes to practice Loving Awareness Meditation before each session with a mute child in order to calm herself down and raise her ability to be present. She commented, "The breath allows me to feel connected to the bigger field of life, which we all are part of."

Then I suggested that when she was confronted with those wordless children and their often frustrated mothers, she do the Heart that Cares for All Practice. "You could imagine the mothers and daughters along with the little girl you once were."

Almost inaudibly, Heidi said,

- May all be included, the immigrant children, their mothers, my mother, and myself in my loving care.
- And, just as I am committed to waking up and finding freedom, I include the well-being and freedom of those frightened children in my caring as well.
- May all immigrants and refugees of this world find safety, support, and loving shelter.

She concluded the practice with,

- May we all be happy.
- May we all be safe.
- May we all receive the support and care we need.
- May we all be free.

Heidi felt the deep wish that she, as both a person and a therapist, could make a difference to those children, that she could help them to become happier and freer than she had been herself. She later told me that this way of working so gently and nonjudgmentally with her emotions had helped her to be more loving and effective as a family therapist. As she became more and more aware of her previously unconscious feelings, she became increasingly able to be with her clients with clarity, wisdom, and care.

Heidi's story can show you how your old and ingrained wounds, including those that have been passed down by generations before you, can be healed with a careful combination of Western and Buddhist psychology. Western methods of counseling can help you to meet trauma by teaching you to listen carefully to the particular resonance of your wound. This allows you to remember and mourn what has happened to you.

Often terror or anger can arise as you emerge from a place of being frozen or numb. Practices from Buddhist psychology can help you to meet those feelings completely without judgment, with gentleness and patience. That allows you to accept what has happened in the past instead of becoming defensive. Loving Awareness Meditation helped Heidi to stay grounded in her body and her feelings.

With Loving Awareness Meditation, you can experience the *now*, the present moment, as refuge and a touch point you can always come back to at any time. The gentle and warm out-breath in this meditation signals you to experience emotional and physical warmth with each exhalation. The Self-Compassion Practice allowed Heidi to hold her painful experience with warmth and tenderness. With the help of compassion practice, you become your own agent for healing. Loving Awareness Meditation, the Self-Compassion Practice, and the Heart That Cares for All Practice helped to transform the wounds that had been passed down through generations of Heidi's family and allowed her to bring healing to the next generation.

RELATED PRACTICES

Loving Awareness Meditation—Chapter 7, pages 43–44
The Self-Compassion Practice—Chapter 10, page 68
The Compassion for Others Practice—Chapter 11, pages 78–79
The Heart that Cares for All (Bodhichitta) Practice—Chapter 12, pages 88–89

JOURNAL EXERCISE

Sit down with a pencil and paper in a quiet place. Make yourself comfortable, rest in your gentle breath, and see what images and stories arise as you read the following prompts. If your own experiences come to mind, do some free writing.

1. Think of a painful pattern in your life, a way of being and relating, that may have its origin in your childhood. Engage in free writing about this.
2. Imagine how this painful pattern could transform through the practice of mindfulness and compassion. Describe what could change.
3. Imagine what would happen if you would bring the Self-Compassion, Compassion for Others, and Heart That Cares for All practices into this predicament.

19

When You Feel Betrayed

This is the story of a lost friendship, which forced me to face feelings of deep hurt and betrayal. The Mindful Pause and the Spiral of Compassion and Forgiveness practices helped me to respond skillfully rather than react in destructive ways. Through the Spiral of Compassion and Forgiveness Practice, I gradually transformed my wound.

Joel had been my best friend since I first came to San Francisco in the mideighties. We both had gone to school to study psychology. Together we had wondered about the big questions in life, such as what is truly meaningful and what can heal suffering. He was a Dominican monk with a love for mindfulness meditation, and I was a Buddhist and, in my heart, a bit of a nun; we both longed to dedicate our lives to what was most essential to us spiritually.

In the late eighties of San Francisco, we co-led a group for men who were suffering from AIDS. For almost three years, we hosted this group of mostly young and middle-aged men. We wept together and attended countless funerals as the members of our group died suddenly and much too early. We had a shared understanding due to our Catholic backgrounds and our love for Buddhist meditation. We loved to discuss how both paths could flow together and help to make our world a kinder and more compassionate place.

After we had been friends for seven years, one early fall evening, Joel asked me if I could help the Dominicans by serving on one of their boards in my function as a psychologist. My task would be to find help for those who had been abused by some of the Dominican friars. Many of the victims had been minors when the abuse happened. I ended up serving on this review board for twelve years, listening to countless stories of abuse, evaluating victims, and finding help for those who had been hurt. As part of my assignment, I developed spiritual healing retreats for victims and their families with the goal of allowing them to find support from each other.

Several years after I had joined the board, Joel was advanced unexpectedly in his monastic order and ended up becoming the supervisor of our lay consulting board. What our group did not know was that he had received the mandate to eliminate our board.

As there were signs that the values and priorities of our mission were about to change along with the new leadership, I became afraid of losing my friendship with Joel. When I saw him, he seemed different, more distant. Hoping that meditating together would safeguard our friendship, I accompanied Joel on several meditation retreats. For a while, this created a thin veneer of closeness. Yet as much as Joel and I loved each other, the pull of opposing interest groups created more and more tension in our friendship.

When there was finally a confrontation over the direction of the board, Joel chose loyalty to his institution. He abruptly withdrew his support. From then on, there was only a chilly distance between us. Even though I understood why Joel had made his choice, I felt the excruciating pain of disappointment and abandonment, which reminded me of the times when I had felt forsaken and rejected during my childhood. It felt again as if my father had left a note: "I do not want to see the child."

I saw my old wounds become inflamed. Ongoing mindfulness and compassion practices helped me hold the anguish I was experiencing. Slowly the hurt lessened and gave way to compassion for myself, for Joel, and even for the terrified and threatened religious institution to which he belonged.

However, my pain kept coming up through the years that followed, especially when something reminded me of Joel. When a common friend inquired about Joel, it sent me off into an inner spin of reactivity. This is when my practices became crucially important to me. Right in the moment when thoughts of Joel were reactivated, the brief Mindful Pause Practice helped me to trace my way out of my swirling mind to find solid ground again.

⟜ THE MINDFUL PAUSE PRACTICE

When I Feel Triggered

1. I notice my body.
2. I choose to pause.
3. I exhale gently to relax.
4. I feel my feelings.
5. I sense my heart.
6. I offer compassion to myself.
7. When I am ready, I reengage.

Doing this practice interrupted my churning thoughts and feelings and allowed me to find my equanimity again, especially at times when my heart felt reinjured by incidental news. Noticing the sensation in my body helped me to feel grounded again. Making a choice to take a pause supported my desire to redirect my unruly mind and heart. It was important to experience my feelings, as this allowed me to feel understood and recognized in my suffering. Experiencing the felt sense of my thoughts and emotions kept me from spiraling in my mind. I also realized that transformation was possible in the present moment of the felt sense. Offering compassion for myself allowed me to find the center in my heart and to feel less afraid. Instead I felt a sense of warmth and calm. Consciously surrendering to the flow of my breath made it possible for me to leave the anguished place of feeling lost in separateness and to experience myself as part of a greater whole.

Meditating regularly and repeating the Mindful Pause Practice over and over, I learned that I could bring awareness and choice to the painful situation with Joel. Most of all, I learned intimately about many of my difficult emotions and realized that they were nobody's responsibility but my own. As I looked inward, I saw fear, shame, and rage, and I had to stare them in the face. Increasingly I learned to turn my gaze inward with fearlessness.

Yet I realized that I would frequently go two steps forward and one step back, that I had to return to my practices with vigilance and humility. Gradually I saw a pattern to my reactivity.

Many of you may have such internal patterns of hurt, yet they vary in their themes. These old structures—which Jungians call complexes, Buddhists call *samskaras*, and I call painfully recurrent patterns—are often hidden to you. Most of the time you are not even aware they exist. When you inadvertently touch on one of them, you are often surprised by your huge emotional and physical reaction. Meditation teacher Pema Chödrön suggests that we all have "propensities to be bothered,"[1] meaning that we have preexisting patterns that make us suffer. My experience with Joel touched one such old pattern of abandonment and betrayal that had slumbered in the depths of my psyche.

I also followed the steps of the Spiral of Compassion and Forgiveness Practice in healing the entrenched distress I had experienced with Joel. On several occasions, I had found myself fantasizing that "all of my enemies" would feel as badly hurt as I did. One day, a local client asked me about my work on the review board. A painful memory surfaced to haunt me—the whole leading council of the institution, monks in their habits, facing me with stern eyes and telling me that my view of the situation was completely false. The atmosphere seemed medieval and scary, and I felt utterly rejected and disgraced. Just the memory of this moment brought chills to the back of my torso and arms. I decided to try the Spiral of Compassion and Forgiveness Practice.

When I got home that evening, I sat in a comfortable meditation position and focused my attention on the sensation and flow of my breath. My mind calmed down and gained some degree of concentration. As I started to look inward, I realized how much hurt I still felt even after so many years.

I began to offer compassion to myself and to hold my sadness, anger, and humiliation with gentle attention. The contraction in the area of my heart loosened. I felt how disappointed I was in myself. How did I let this get so bad? I realized that I needed to forgive myself.

I longed to accept myself in this situation just the way I was. I am not perfect, I make mistakes, and I am human. Things will turn out the way they will.

Then I thought of all those others who are in conflict with a powerful institution, culture, or government. I also thought of all those who had lost friends for many reasons—illness, death, disagreement, or betrayal. I sent loving-kindness to this whole group of people.

Now the practice became more challenging. Would I be able to send compassion to Joel and his monastic order? I had an agreement with myself, that if sincere positive feelings now proved too difficult, I could hold the aspiration that maybe in ten years I would develop a sense of warmth and caring for those by whom I had felt hurt. This would allow me, or so I hoped, to crack open the door.

As I was holding Joel in my mind, I was astonished to realize that I actually did feel some compassion for him. I recognized how squeezed in the middle he must have felt in a no-win situation, how sad he must have felt during that time and maybe now. As I turned my attention to the clerics in his order, I imagined that they must have felt under attack by the public and activist groups. My heart went out to them.

But I had not forgiven Joel, and I had not forgiven the clerics. Reassuring myself that to forgive does not mean to condone, I put the intention forward to forgive gradually. Forgiveness, I was coming to understand, means to let go of a grudge.

During the time I worked with the Spiral of Compassion and Forgiveness Practice, I realized that I needed to work with it over and over. I continued the following phrases as part of my morning meditations:

- May I forgive you, who I feel hurt by.
- May you forgive me, as I have hurt you.
- May I forgive myself for the pain I caused to others and myself.

Slowly my heart began to open up and soften. The group of monks came to my mind's eye as they were flooded with lawsuits. I realized how understandable the group's defensiveness was. Being afraid of bankruptcy, the monks were worried about how to sustain their own elderly friars.

At the same time, images arose of an abuse survivor I had known, who had been hurt through his trust in authority, church, and God. Alcohol had been his refuge for many years, until the church finally paid for rehab. Then I saw images of my friend Joel, uncomfortable, stressed, and scared, and how betwixt and between he must have felt, so torn in his loyalties. As I opened my heart to him, I realized that for the past several years he must have lived with tremendous pressure and tension.

The Spiral of Compassion and Forgiveness Practice helped me to hold this complex potpourri of feelings, memories, and opinions that make up our human suffering. I prayed that my practices would help me to cultivate a heart that was wide enough to hold this suffering with wisdom and compassion.

It seemed natural to me now to expand my well-wishing to all those who live in times of disagreement, conflict, or war—to all humans, all animals, and the world.

Physically my heart felt as if it had stretched, as if it had more space inside to hold all that needed to be held. In fact I felt a sense of gratitude that I would not be stuck forever with my awful resentments and feelings of disgrace and shame. I felt grateful that I was beginning to feel more at peace with my lost friendship with Joel and, at the same time, open to change should there be a new chance for caring and forgiveness.

RELATED PRACTICES

The Mindful Pause Practice—Chapter 8, page 51
The Spiral of Compassion and Forgiveness Practice—Chapter 14, pages
  111–12

JOURNAL EXERCISE

Sit down with a pencil and paper in a quiet place. Make yourself comfortable, rest in your gentle breath, and see what images and stories arise as you read the following prompts. If your own experiences come to mind, do some free writing.

1. Describe a time in your life when you lost a friendship or other relationship that was important to you. Do some free writing about this.
2. Imagine that you could scroll back the movie of your memories. Reenvision the turn of events if you had been able to take a mindful pause. Describe the outcome.
3. Reenvision the turn of events if you had been able to work through the Spiral of Compassion and Forgiveness Practice. How might that have influenced your wounded relationship?

20

When Money Problems Threaten Your Relationship

This is the story of a loving couple made up of two strong individuals whose financial stresses almost tore them apart. So often when our lives already feel burdened, worry about money is the straw that breaks the camel's back. In my work with this couple, I encouraged them to return to ongoing Mindfulness Meditation, which allowed them to slow down, to recognize the danger they were in, and to seek appropriate help. Besides their daily Mindfulness Meditation and Loving Awareness Meditation, both partners also engaged in the When There Is Tension and Hurt between a Couple practice, making it possible to face each other with wisdom and compassion during this time of stress.

Jasmine, a beautiful brunette in her early fifties, wearing fashionable black-rimmed glasses and colorful shawls, looked exasperated. Thomas, a tall, handsome man with penetrating green eyes, buried his face in his hands. Jasmine looked at me with pleading eyes. "Can you help us? I'm afraid to lose the man I love. This money stress is turning us into enemies."

Thomas said in a subdued voice, "We can't afford our life anymore, and everything may just fall apart."

Jasmine chimed in, "You should have known that earlier . . ."

Both of them caught themselves and looked at me expectantly.

I said, "I'd like to hear what's going on. With increased understanding and some practices in mindful communication, we might be able to untangle the mess you're experiencing. However, I recommend that we do a brief Loving Awareness Meditation for five minutes before you tell me your story."

Jasmine sighed and closed her eyes; her shoulders dropped an inch or two, and her face began to soften. After some moments of quiet breathing, Thomas's hands relaxed in his lap. I guided them: "Let yourself settle into the sensations in your body and feel your feet touching the ground." Gradually, the energy in my office seemed to calm down.

I continued, "With kindness, allow yourself to recognize what is going on in your body, where you feel tight, where you feel pressure or numbness, lightness or heaviness." Then I instructed them to feel the sensations and movements of their natural breath and, while following their breath, to allow their bodies to be breathed. They seemed to nestle a little more deeply into their chairs as they relaxed a bit further with each out-breath. I added, "Allow yourself to experience a quality of warmth, of caring with your out-breath, and with each exhalation, let go a little more, sink a little deeper." The Loving Awareness Meditation connected the warmth of the flow of breath with a feeling of friendliness and reassurance. When I rang the bell after five minutes, both of them seemed more settled and less volatile.

Fifteen years earlier, Thomas and Jasmine had met at a conference in Mexico City. Jasmine was living in the States and was employed as a political science professor. She had emigrated from Egypt twelve years before that to marry an American man of Egyptian heritage. That marriage had fallen apart and ended after the kids were born, as Jasmine had become increasingly independent and confident in herself.

When they met, Thomas, a Brazilian lawyer and specialist in international law, was living in Sao Paulo, Brazil. He was separated from his wife, with whom he shared custody of children who were in their teens. At the human rights conference in Mexico City, Thomas and Jasmine fell in love. The following year, Thomas managed to move from Brazil to America to be with Jasmine. This required navigating a lot of complications due to his immigration status and the necessity of relicensing as a US lawyer.

At the time when Thomas and Jasmine met, they shared five children between them. Jasmine's two girls and a boy were nine, seven, and four, respectively. Thomas's two boys were a bit older. To be together, Thomas had to change continents, leaving behind his job as well as his household. Both his and Jasmine's lives were turned upside down.

Their passion for each other was strong. Both shared interests in legal and political issues, especially around restorative justice in war-stricken countries. They also shared spiritual interests in the practice of mindfulness and ethics. They could talk about social, political, and spiritual themes without ever getting tired of each other.

Once they had settled together in Santa Barbara, it took Thomas and Jasmine several years to earn enough to afford a mortgage. Blending their two families had been quite a challenge, but over time the lively, colorful family grew together. Even though Thomas's boys lived with their mother, they visited during the school holidays.

Thomas and Jasmine's problems arose when their finances crumbled. Both had been used to comfortable lifestyles in their previous marriages and professions, and both had brought with them an assumption that there would always be enough money. Now finances were very tight, including the expenses associated with paying for five children and professional reestablishment. The couple experienced a lot of stress during Thomas's time of unemployment, until he was able to pass the California bar exam, which allowed him to work as a lawyer in the United States.

Then the couple met a new fiscal challenge, but they still did not know how to communicate about finances. They continued patterns they had learned from their parents of living beyond their means and spending generously. Their arrangement had worked during the economic boom, when house prices went up and they could take equity out of their property to fund their lifestyle. As the economy changed and their financial affairs worsened, however, Thomas and Jasmine avoided talking about money issues; in fact, they evaded difficult dialogues altogether. Life seemed complicated enough without stirring the pot.

When they could no longer pay their mortgage, they had to move to a smaller house. However, their unhealthy spending habits and lack of communication remained. Finally their situation became critical when they received a huge unexpected tax bill. Both of them were swinging from panic to despondency. In their pain, they accused each other of bad decisions in the past and began to blame each other.

Jasmine's fear of not being able to bring up her kids in a secure way felt overwhelming. Her pain was so devastating that she couldn't find refuge in the meditation practice that had helped her in the past. Thomas, who was able to remain steadier, was unable to console her. Jasmine often woke in a panic in the middle of the night. The morning after a particularly frightening panic attack, she called me to ask if they could see me together.

During the following week, they came to my office. I saw the usually vibrant couple walking down the path looking a bit ragged. I listened and understood how this current problem had developed and how now was the time for them to get a grip on their finances as well as their relationship.

Both of them sat awkwardly in their chairs, looking at each other with some misgiving. "You should have known better," she challenged.

"And why did you not participate in planning our finances?" he shot back.

"You're looking out more for your kids in Brazil than for us here," she said.

"And you are spending too much on yourself and your kids' clothes," he said.

"I do not feel supported by you, and don't know what to do anymore," she said.

"And there is nothing I can say that will reassure you. You insist on being in this black hole and blaming me for all that is wrong here," he summed up.

As their therapist, I saw them going down a path toward hopelessness and an entrenched pattern of miscommunication. I had an idea and intervened. "Can we have a pause, please? How about engaging in an exercise together. I will guide you through a practice: When There Is Tension and Hurt between Couples and Pairs. But let's start with some attention to breath again, so we can get grounded." They looked at each other in an exasperated way; then they shrugged their shoulders and said, "Okay."

WHEN THERE IS TENSION AND HURT BETWEEN COUPLES AND PAIRS PRACTICE

Each person should relax in a chair and engage with the following practice:

1. I notice the energy in the room.
2. I sense my body.
3. I choose to pause.
4. I exhale gently to relax.
5. I feel the breath of my heart.
6. I generate compassion for myself.
7. I let myself be open to feel the other's energy.
8. I allow compassion for the other.
9. I return to the stream of breath that connects us all.
10. When I am ready, I reengage.

As we went through the practice, I suggested that they notice the sensations in their bodies and feel the contact of their feet on the floor, the touch of their buttocks on the chairs. Then I asked them to feel the energy in the room. When we reflected later in the session, Jasmine reported that she had felt the tension and hostility between them, and Thomas said that he had noticed their defensiveness standing between them.

In the third step in the practice, I encouraged them to press a metaphorical pause button, with the color and texture of their choice. Later Jasmine shared that her pause button was blue-green and made out of fine Arabian silk. Thomas imagined his pause button in the jungles of Brazil as a blue pool of water, one he could dive into.

In step 4, I suggested that they each take three deep breaths, feel the sensation of breath, and let go with their out-breaths. I saw how both of their jaws were softening and how their shoulders dropped down. Both of them reported after the exercise that feeling the gentle sensation of breath had helped them to come back to the present moment.

In step 5, I suggested that they sense the air brushing through the area of their hearts, like a warm wind would lightly brush through the leaves of a willow. I encouraged them to feel what was going on in their hearts. "Sometimes one might feel tightness or constriction, a bit of an ache or numbness, lightness or heaviness," I offered.

Jasmine told us after the exercise was over that she had felt a sense of rawness and ache inside her chest in the area of her heart. Thomas reported that he had felt mere numbness and an uncomfortable sense of coldness.

In step 6, I encouraged both of them to allow for a feeling of compassion, of caring for themselves. Each needed to honor his or her own history and predicament with acceptance and warmth. Tears rolled down Jasmine's cheeks, and she began rubbing the area of her heart with her right hand. Thomas's face became a bit softer, and his breathing became subtle.

Jasmine later told me that images of the many perils in her life had passed through her mind during this exercise. Like images in a river, she saw faces—her father's, her ex-husband's, Thomas's, her children's, and her own face as a little girl. Thomas told me that a feeling of compassion for himself was new to him but that he had felt a touch of softness and caring for himself and for the challenges he was facing in his current life.

In step 7, I asked each of them to allow for openness to the other's experience and to feel what the other might be feeling. They sat quietly for a long while in a tender kind of way.

Later Jasmine reported that she felt Thomas's exhaustion and worry for the family. Her heart went out to him. Thomas told her that he sensed her vulnerability and her fear of losing her home again, as she had when she left Egypt and when her first marriage had ended. He also sensed her fear of getting old in a foreign and cold place. As they shared these empathetic thoughts, he reached for her hand.

In step 9, I suggested that they both return to the ground of breath, feel the sensation of breath brushing through, and allow for the feeling that their bodies were being breathed. I encouraged them to sense breath brushing out as they exhaled and flowing in as they inhaled and to experience their interdependence through the flow of breath.

Both of them later recalled that returning to the ground of breath had allowed them to sense more fluidity and spaciousness, even in their rigidly held emotions and beliefs. Feeling their own hurts and imagining what the other might be experiencing brought them to a place of softening and understanding toward each other. Both reported that they now felt part of a bigger whole—with each other and with something larger, the whole breathing world.

After we had completed the steps of the When There Is Tension and Hurt between Couples and Pairs Practice, I asked both of them if they felt ready to reengage. They nodded quietly. They looked at me and then at each other and smiled. That is when they shared the internal experiences they had had during the meditation. They talked for a long time. They cried a bit and held each other's hands at times. Then they looked at me as Jasmine announced, "I think we can go forward from here. There's hope now."

I was reminded of Buddhist teacher Sharon Salzberg's words: "We need to have faith in our practice. When we keep practicing, doors will open eventually."[2]

RELATED PRACTICES

Loving Awareness Meditation—Chapter 7, pages 43–44
When There Is Tension and Hurt between a Couple—Chapter 15, page
*   131*

JOURNAL EXERCISE

Sit down with a pencil and paper in a quiet place. Make yourself comfortable, rest in your gentle breath, and see what images and stories arise as you read the following prompts. If your own experiences come to mind, do some free writing.

1. Remember a time when stresses, such as money, workload, or other external hardships, challenged your life's balance. How did you feel? What effect did these external hardships have on your relationships? Reflect. Do some free writing about this.
2. Describe yourself doing a practice you regard as helpful in a situation where you try to keep your inner balance despite considerable external stressors.
3. Take the Compassionate Choice for Couples. Imagine and describe a sequence with someone with whom you are close but in conflict.

21

When Rage Threatens to Destroy Your Life

This story is about Gregory, who had to face his tendency to react with anger and sometimes rage when he was triggered. With the help of Mindfulness Meditation, Loving Awareness Meditation, and the Compassionate Choice Practice, he was able to bring awareness to his reactivity and slow down his impulsivity. With these newfound skills, he was able to move forward without allowing his rage and aggression to sabotage his life.

Many of you learned hurtful ways of relating from your parents and your environment, or you developed unskillful habits to cope with hard times. These ways of behaving may have gotten you in trouble early on, or they may have served you when you were little but have now become obsolete, even destructive.

Your anger may have been born of trauma or situations in which you were treated without respect and love. Many of us have learned that anger is a way to make our desires known. Unknowingly, you may continue to react to triggers in ways that do not serve you. With ongoing

Mindfulness Meditation and a range of other practices that bring awareness and compassion to the present moment, you can learn how to face
what is hard to look at and transform hurtful patterns of reacting into
healthier ways of being, both with yourself and when responding to
others.

Gregory, who started out as a skinny, sandy-blond Irish boy with per-
suasive brown eyes, grew up under miserable conditions in a rundown
area of Boston. There he lived with a bitter and resentful mom, as well an
older brother who teased him and beat him up, all under the tyranny of
an alcoholic and violent stepdad. In Gregory's family, there had been a
long history of violence and distress. The men in the family had a long-
standing tradition of being successful street fighters and were proud of
Gregory's great-grandfather, who had been a much-admired Northern
Irish revolutionary.

When Gregory's parents divorced early on, Gregory ended up living
with his mom. As a little boy, he suffered frequent beatings by his
drunken stepfather and unruly older brother. Secretly, Gregory idolized
his biological father, a poet and fisherman known for "standing his
ground" when challenged.

Gregory himself was known to get mad and even enraged. By the time
I met him, he was twenty-six years old. He was the foreman in a con-
struction company, a tall, muscular guy with surfer-blond hair and
penetrating eyes. Women regarded him as attractive, and men tended to
see him as intimidating. Over the years, Gregory had had several court
appearances for, as he put it, "defending friends." Even though he had
never ended up in prison, he'd had to appear in court repeatedly because
of having hurt people in serious fights.

When I began to work with him, I was not sure whether Gregory would
have the courage and patience to tolerate facing his own rage and be able
to speak of his bone-deep anxiety and self-doubt that I assumed was there.
Yet, in spite of his past and current challenges, Gregory always had a
deep longing to give meaning to his life and to support others in having a
better chance to live healthier lives than the one he had experienced

growing up. An innate desire to grow inspired Gregory to ask for help and to start transforming his destructive patterns.

In working with me, he learned to meditate and was trying to keep up a daily practice. During our sessions, he and I had sometimes followed the steps of the Compassionate Choice Practice. He was making some progress in developing awareness and in choosing to respond rationally rather than react in anger. At the end of the first year we worked together, he received an invitation to do a graduate degree in urban planning at MIT with a full scholarship, but he was afraid that one of his impending court cases might make that impossible.

One morning, I received an urgent phone call from Gregory, asking for an appointment to come to my office as soon as possible. He had come extremely close to a fistfight with a neighborhood watchman. In a dispute over the use of a garbage container, the two men had become so enraged that only the intervention of a friend had prevented physical violence. His friend had had to drag away a kicking and screaming Gregory. The watchman called the police.

To make things worse, Gregory had a court case pending from a year earlier. He had knocked a man out during an intoxicated fistfight at a bar. If this complaint from the watchman ended up in court, it was certain that Gregory's record would swing the courts against him.

Sitting in my office chair, Gregory ruffled his hair. Then he burrowed his head into his hands and looked at me with an exasperated expression on his face. "This watchman guy is an asshole," he said.

"Ready to work?" I countered.

Having done the Compassionate Choice Practice before, Gregory was now able to track the cascade of his reactions. As I was reading the definitions of the consecutive steps, he responded, describing his own experience.

Compassionate Choice Practice

TRIGGER
Something happens that sparks an immediate uncomfortable feeling. This trigger can be set off by internal thoughts and feelings or by external events.

SENSATION
Our body responds instantaneously. We may experience, for example, a tightening in our belly, a constriction near our heart, or a flushed face.

EMOTION
Feelings that come up may be anger, fear, sadness, embarrassment, indignation, or some other unpleasant emotion.

AUTOMATIC ASSOCIATION
Moods, memories, and images from our past arise and entangle us and intensify emotions.

EMOTIONAL CONCLUSION
Consciously or unconsciously, we form beliefs about ourselves, others, and our world which seem convincing.

URGE TO ACT
We experience a great deal of tension, which can be externalized as an intense desire to fix the situation or internalized as intense rumination.

Mindful Time-Out

We choose to interrupt the reactive process with an activity that restores our inner balance. We notice the sensations and emotions of more tenderness and quiet.

COMPASSIONATE AWARENESS
We notice our reaction to the trigger with compassion for ourselves and others.

SENSATIONS & EMOTIONS OF COMPASSION
We feel the sensations and emotions when expanding our care to ourselves and others.

COMPASSIONATE EVALUATION
We gain a wider perspective and can consider a range of possibilities.

COMPASSIONATE CHOICE
We respond with more awareness, skill, and care.

RESULTING SENSATIONS & EMOTIONS
We feel the sensations and emotions having made a compassionate choice. We may feel increased relaxation, physical wellness, aliveness, and an improved connection with others.

OUTCOME
New response patterns can develop and our relationship to ourselves and others improve.

Trigger

Gregory was aware that the watchman's criticism of him and the seeming unfairness had felt like an attack and set off the cascade of his reactivity.

Sensation

When he recalled the situation, Gregory sensed an extremely tense feeling in his arms and shoulders as well as in his jaw. He also reported having felt a thick knot in his stomach.

Emotions

Gregory was aware of how outraged he had become. However, after gaining some awareness, he became increasingly alarmed by how strong his reaction against the watchman had been.

Automatic Association

A barrage of images, feelings, and memories flooded Gregory. He remembered the many times when he had become involved in fights. Images came up from when he had been severely beaten by his stepfather and older brother.

Emotional Conclusion

Gregory noticed two contradictory, strongly held beliefs within himself. One was that the world was full of dangerous men who had to be fended off and kept down. The other was that he, like every man in his family, would end up in jail one day, defeated by life.

Urge to Act

Gregory was ruminating endlessly over possible payback to this watchman. He reported fantasies of going over to where the watchman lived and beating him "to a pulp."

Mindful Time-Out

I reminded Gregory that an alternative to careening down the reactive pathway would be to slow down and become aware of what was going on. I suggested that he take an extended Mindful Time-Out, a break in which he could interrupt the reactive process and rebalance himself. The weekend was approaching, and I recommended that he take a full day to work with himself. "The possibility of making mindful choices will be much higher if you take this time-out," I reminded him. We also agreed that he would stay away from the watchman until our next visit.

On the following Sunday, Gregory turned his phone off. Before breakfast, he did a five-mile run. After a long, warm shower, he already felt a lot less tense. Then he ate a light breakfast on his own, in silence, without news and music. During this Mindful Time-Out, he found particular relief from chaotic angry thoughts when he engaged in the practice of Mindfulness Meditation with focus on the out-breath. Gregory sat on a wooden chair. With a cushion supporting his back, he sat straight with his feet touching the ground.

∽ MINDFULNESS MEDITATION

- I feel the sensations in my body, between my body and the chair, my feet and the ground.
- I allow my shoulders and jaw to relax.
- I notice the sensation of breath, expanding with the in-breath, letting go with the out-breath.
- I allow my body to be breathed.
- With each out-breath, I let go a bit more.
- When my mind gets distracted, I allow thoughts, feelings, and images to pass by freely.
- I always return to my refuge, my touchstone, the breath.
- I allow myself to surrender to the movement of breath.

Slowly Gregory's body began to relax, and the tightness in his shoulders and jaw began to let go. Gradually his mind became calm enough that he was able to feel the subtle sensation and movement of his breath. When images of the fight with the watchman passed through his mind, at first they carried him away. At one point, he realized after fifteen minutes that he had been caught and carried away by a stressful daydream. He returned to his breath, remembering to be kind instead of irritated with himself. After that he was able to stay connected to his breath a little more closely.

Later that day, for a second meditation, Gregory lay down on the rug. He chose the Loving Awareness Meditation. He knew that kindness toward himself was extremely challenging. He experienced it as almost unbearable to allow the feeling of warmth, including emotional warmth, to brush through the area of his chest. The thought of gentleness felt unmanly to him, allowing far too much vulnerability for his comfort.

However, from our discussions, he had come to realize that he was his own worst enemy and that his thoughts were most violent against himself. So he took on what felt like a manageable task: to do five loving awareness breaths. He thought this would be barely tolerable.

⟿ LOVING AWARENESS MEDITATION

- I settle into the sensations within my body.
- I allow the natural breath to flow through: expanding with the in-breath, letting go with the out-breath.
- I notice the felt sense within my heart and I feel the gentle sensation of the out-breath brush through.
- With each out-breath, I connect to a sense of warmth and caring.
- When I get distracted, I connect to the sensation of gentleness in my out-breath.
- For a while, I stay with this sensation of loving awareness.

Very slowly, Gregory followed the sensation of breath as it flowed through his heart. Breath touching his heart felt like sun melting ice or touch meeting numbness. For five minutes, he was able to engage in the loving awareness breath. With his stance toward himself now turning a bit gentler, he recognized how hard his life had been for so many years.

In the afternoon, he sat down and finished the second half of the Compassionate Choice Practice. As he looked through the worksheet, he wrote his responses in the chart, following step-by-step.

Compassionate Choice Practice Worksheet

TRIGGER

```
┌─────────────────────────────────────────────┐
│                                             │
│                                             │
│                                             │
└─────────────────────────────────────────────┘
```

SENSATION

```
┌─────────────────────────────────────────────┐
│                                             │
│                                             │
│                                             │
└─────────────────────────────────────────────┘
```

EMOTION

```
┌─────────────────────────────────────────────┐
│                                             │
│                                             │
│                                             │
└─────────────────────────────────────────────┘
```

AUTOMATIC ASSOCIATION

```
┌─────────────────────────────────────────────┐
│                                             │
│                                             │
│                                             │
└─────────────────────────────────────────────┘
```

EMOTIONAL CONCLUSION

```
┌─────────────────────────────────────────────┐
│                                             │
│                                             │
│                                             │
└─────────────────────────────────────────────┘
```

URGE TO ACT

```
┌─────────────────────────────────────────────┐
│                                             │
│                                             │
│                                             │
└─────────────────────────────────────────────┘
```

Mindful Time-Out

```
┌──────────────────────────────────────────────┐
│                                                │
│                                                │
│                                                │
└──────────────────────────────────────────────┘
```

COMPASSIONATE AWARENESS

```
┌──────────────────────────────────────────────┐
│                                                │
│                                                │
│                                                │
└──────────────────────────────────────────────┘
```

SENSATIONS & EMOTIONS OF COMPASSION

```
┌──────────────────────────────────────────────┐
│                                                │
│                                                │
│                                                │
└──────────────────────────────────────────────┘
```

COMPASSIONATE EVALUATION

```
┌──────────────────────────────────────────────┐
│                                                │
│                                                │
│                                                │
└──────────────────────────────────────────────┘
```

COMPASSIONATE CHOICE

```
┌──────────────────────────────────────────────┐
│                                                │
│                                                │
│                                                │
└──────────────────────────────────────────────┘
```

RESULTING SENSATIONS & EMOTIONS

```
┌──────────────────────────────────────────────┐
│                                                │
│                                                │
│                                                │
└──────────────────────────────────────────────┘
```

OUTCOME

```
┌──────────────────────────────────────────────┐
│                                                │
│                                                │
│                                                │
└──────────────────────────────────────────────┘
```

Compassionate Awareness

Gregory now understood how his early experiences with his stepfather and older brother had shaped his predilection for violent responses. With empathy, he also remembered the little boy who had been dragged to countless court battles between his mother and father.

Compassionate Evaluation

With this increased understanding, he could hold a wider perspective to evaluate the situation anew. Gregory recognized now that only with great luck had he been able to avoid past criminal charges. It became clear to him that if he wanted to go to graduate school, his violent temper plus a criminal record would be a huge impediment. He also began to realize that it would not really make him happy inside to take revenge on the watchman. Holding a broader perspective, he now understood that it would take a lot of work to develop new ways of responding. At the same time, his resolve to make a different life for himself became even stronger.

Compassionate Choice

Gregory decided to come to therapy twice a week in the coming months and commit to an hour of meditation every day. He also committed himself to stay away from the watchman for a minimum of three months.

After this Mindful Time-Out, Gregory felt very tired. Yet he also felt happier inside and went to bed early.

When he came to his next therapy session, he was eager to show me the chart he had filled out the Sunday before. Being able to put his internal processes down on paper, facilitated by the format of the Compassionate Choice Practice chart, allowed Gregory to feel more organized and less out of control. By working with himself patiently and diligently in the coming months, he started to feel more and more relief. The following fall, when he began graduate school at MIT, he found a therapist on campus and joined a meditation group.

If you, like Gregory, have a recurrent painful pattern that has troubled your life for a long time, reactive behaviors may continue to occur even when you have worked to change them. For example, I still feel hurt when I feel excluded or judged by others. But now, after working with the Mindful Pause Practice, the Compassionate Choice Practice, and the Spiral of Compassion and Forgiveness Practice, my internal "heart and mind storms" do not have to lead to destructive actions. Like me, Gregory, and many other people whose stories are shared here, you can learn to respond rather than react, which leads to a healthier and happier life. Having developed yourself in this way, you can also learn to serve your world more effectively.

RELATED PRACTICES

The Compassionate Choice Practice—Chapter 13, page 95
Mindfulness Meditation—Chapter 7, pages 40–41
Loving Awareness Meditation—Chapter 7, pages 43–44

JOURNAL EXERCISE

Sit down with a pencil and paper in a quiet place. Make yourself comfortable, rest in your gentle breath, and see what images and stories arise as you read the following prompts. Do some free writing about one of the three scenarios.

1. Think about an area of impulsivity in your life. You may have a tendency to get angry and full of rage, or you may have other impulsive ways of releasing tension such as overeating, buying what you don't need, or getting intoxicated. Do some free writing about this.
2. Go through the Compassionate Choice practice step-by-step and imagine how you could have reacted differently to an event that triggered you to act impulsively.
3. Imagine a few times when a mindful pause might work for you. Describe one and imagine how your experience might unfold step-by-step if you took on this practice.

22

When Self-Hate Turns You against Yourself and Others

This is the story of a girl who grew up as a boy. Loraine went down a painful path as her body transitioned from male to female. Besides the physical challenges she encountered, she had to work through feelings of self-hatred and alienation toward the person, the male child and teenager, she had been before. Her delicate steps in facing her thoughts and feelings and gradually allowing for self-compassion to develop helped her make peace with the person she had been, the person she was now, and the person she would become in the future. On this path she made use of the Heart's Intention Practice as well as the Self-Compassion and Compassion for Others practices.

When I first began to work with the twenty-one-year-old blond with marine-blue lowlights, she sat down awkwardly in the big, brown leather chair in my office and seemed to struggle with how to position her long, muscular arms and legs. "My surgery will be in seven months," Loraine told me. "Can you write a letter for me stating that I am emotionally fit for this?"

I imagined how much courage it must have taken to ask me for this letter, not to mention the bravery it took to undertake such a huge surgery. "I imagine I can," I answered, "but let's get to know each other first."

I learned that Loraine had grown up as Lucas in the San Fernando Valley and that as a little boy, Lucas had always envied his two older sisters for being girls. He was happiest when his sisters dressed him up in their pretty dresses. He sat extra still as they applied makeup to his face, including blush and mascara. He could not stop staring into the mirror, fantasizing about what it would be like if he could always be like that: a girl. However, when his father came home, he did not like the sight of his little son dressed up as girl. "Stop with that silliness," he chided. Quietly and swiftly, Lucas would wash off the makeup, feeling embarrassed. When it was time to roughhouse with other boys on the soccer field, he felt as if he were playing a role that did not really fit him, yet he awkwardly tried to behave like the other boys. He secretly cursed himself and his out-of-place body, which did not seem to match how he felt.

Loraine told me about the day when Lucas read about Chaz Bono, Cher and Sony Bono's transgender daughter, in one of his sister's magazines. His heart began to beat faster. "That's it," he thought to himself, "that's me." At about fifteen, Lucas slid into a depression, feeling out of place and awkward no matter where he went, and hiding in his room most of the time. "I hate this body," he muttered to himself constantly. His mother, a teacher who knew about kids, finally took him to a psychologist. With the help of Dr. S., Lucas was able to understand that he was, in fact, a girl stuck in a boy's body. With Dr. S.'s support, he was able to tell his parents and sisters about his feelings in a tearful family meeting. His father had the most difficulty in coming on board and accepting that his boy was a girl.

Loraine told her family her true name and said that she would begin dressing as a girl from then on. She felt anger toward her father when he continued to call her Lucas, and she felt hatred toward herself for not being what her father wanted her to be. At night she went around the house and took down pictures of herself as a boy. One evening, she threw the photos in the fireplace and watched them burn.

The day after she burned the photos, she saw a pained look on her mother's face. Her mother had lost her little boy. Loraine felt angry, confused, and at odds with herself and her world. She had hoped that everything would be good now that she had decided to be a girl, dressing and behaving like her sisters. But she was faced with a world of others, including their expectations and hurt feelings. This was important work, and as Loraine readied herself for the surgery, we took a break in meeting.

When I began to see Loraine again a year and a half later, she had gone through an elaborate surgery. Her family, despite their misgivings, and her best friend had given her a certain degree of support. The wounds to her strong, young body were healing quickly.

Yet the injuries to her heart, the subtle estrangement from her father, the silent agony of her mother, and her own feelings of alienation from herself and from the person she had been before the surgery remained. Now that her body had changed, Loraine had hoped she would be able to identify as a gay woman and leave the boy as well as the transgendered person behind.

Even though her body was becoming more and more that of a woman's and she dressed more confidently in expressing who she was, it seemed that the other aspects of her former identity had been left behind too quickly. In our therapy meetings, I likened the situation to "transgender jet lag," where so many changes had happened so fast that her psyche had not had a chance to catch up. The old aspects of herself were hovering in the background like angry left-behind children being told to get lost. I looked for ways that I could support Loraine in finding peace between the different parts that were Loraine/Lucas and to forge compassionate, wise relationships within Loraine and between Loraine and her world.

At first Loraine resisted my peacemaking attempts, insisting that she was now a gay woman and that was that. But as she continued to experience her own pain and to see the suffering of her parents, she softened. Then she had a particularly painful disagreement with her mom. Loraine wanted to destroy all the letters she had written to her mom as a child, as they had been written and signed by Lucas. For Loraine's mother, this signified yet another painful loss.

Loraine asked me, "How can I find peace and create less pain for those I love?" After we talked for a while and explored her inner experience of feeling so divided and her longing to find a sense of integration, I suggested that I would guide her through a brief mindfulness practice, the Heart's Intention Practice.

While Loraine relaxed back into the brown leather chair, I guided her through the following meditation:

- I sense my body.
- I recognize with kindness the passing of thoughts and feelings of self-doubt and confusion.
- I calm my heart with the gentleness of my out-breath.
- I feel with my own suffering and offer compassion to myself.
- I allow breath to move through my body ever so gently, connecting me to the bigger flow of life.
- I recognize my deepest yearning for myself, for my mother, and for the rest of my family.
- I feel the breath of my heart.
- I include others who are also suffering from separation from their families in my prayers.
- I say, "May all of us who feel excluded and divided within ourselves find balance and tender care."
- I allow breath to move through my body, for life to breathe me.

Loraine's body relaxed as she attended to her gentle out-breath, and she sighed deeply. As she felt the degree of her self-doubt and confusion, she realized how much she loved her family and how urgently she wanted to be at peace with them. She also felt reaffirmed in her certainty that she had to live her life authentically, that there was no other choice for her. There had to be a way to reconcile the self she had been with the one in transition and her vision of her future authentic identity.

During our subsequent visits, she began to understand that she would not be able to accept both the boy and the girl inside herself. For now, this had to be an aspiration for the future, which she hoped would become her new reality sooner rather than later. To support her in her aspiration, she began to practice Mindfulness Meditation ten minutes every morning and evening. This time of respite gave her a refuge, a brief time of peace. Together we devised compassion phrases that seemed especially relevant to her situation. Loraine added the following phrases to her evening Self-Compassion Practice:

- May I open my heart to myself and those around me.
- May I offer compassion to myself now and to the boy's body that was my home before.
- May I offer warmth, care, and patience to my body, which had to go through such painful changes.
- May my family and I find a new kind of balance.
- May we all live with love and ease.

As our psychotherapy meetings went on, Loraine realized that much of her suffering was based in shame and guilt. She felt shame about her at-times clumsy, muscular body; about the scars left by her surgery; and about having been a boy. She felt guilty to have caused suffering to her family for being different. We added the following phrases to her meditation:

- May I be free of shame and guilt and all those feelings of embarrassment I harbor.
- May I accept myself for exactly who I am right now.
- May I make friends with the little boy I once was.
- May we all be free.

After I had not heard from Loraine for a year and a half, she came in one day to introduce her girlfriend to me. Loraine and Emma had met at an LBGTQ meditation group in Los Angeles and had moved together to

New York City. Emma worked as a math teacher, and Loraine had become a teacher for autistic children.

Loraine's practice in self-compassion had supported her in making a change that was important in her own life and is essential for many people as they come into their authenticity in this day and age.

RELATED PRACTICES

The Heart's Intention Practice—Chapter 9, pages 58–59
The Self-Compassion Practice—Chapter 10, page 68

JOURNAL EXERCISE

Sit down with a pencil and paper in a quiet place. Make yourself comfortable, rest in your gentle breath, and see what images and stories arise as you read the following prompts. If your own experiences come to mind, do some free writing.

1. Think of a time when you were divided within yourself, and describe how that felt in your body and mind. How did this internal split affect your relationships with others? Do some free writing about this.
2. When you think of the practices presented in this book, which would have helped you regain balance and peace? Think of some self-compassion phrases that would have helped you to make friends with yourself again.

23

When the World's or Another's Suffering Overwhelms You

This is a story about how to practice when you feel overwhelmed by the suffering of another person or the world. There may be times when you feel powerless and can't fix things for others. Practicing mindfulness and self-compassion, specifically the on-the-go practice When I Feel Overwhelmed by the Suffering of Others or Our World, can allow you to find a healthy, stable, and openhearted stance in the midst of difficulty. In addition, even when facing potentially devastating suffering, practicing the Heart That Cares for All Practice can contribute to a wider perspective, providing fulfillment and meaning.

Violetta walked back and forth in her kitchen getting her breakfast ready. The morning light came in through the big window, and the smell of espresso and biscotti gave her a feel of home in California, so far away from her native Colombia. For twenty-five years, Violetta has been teaching climate science at a university in Los Angeles, trying to educate students about the effects of carbon dioxide emissions, greenhouse gasses, and fracking.

Suddenly she noticed a pop-up on the computer beside her breakfast plate. A senior water scientist at NASA's Jet Propulsion Laboratory had published an op-ed in the *Los Angeles Times*: "California has about one year of water left. Will you ration now?" Violetta felt her stomach tighten and experienced a feeling of nausea. This was just the most recent news adding to the vast body of information on the escalating impact of global warming.

She knew right away what the headline meant, not only for Los Angeles, but for California and the wider world. Water was becoming a commodity increasingly in demand, and efforts to access it might well lead to worldwide conflicts.

Later that morning, Violetta sat down to write an article on the relationship between the California drought and global warming. Yet her mind was going around and around in circles, chewing over the facts. Her brain did not want to work, to be creative and lucid. It felt like a wheel desperately stuck in thick mud. As she tried to work, Violetta became more and more frustrated with herself. By evening, she sensed a familiar feeling of depression quietly and insidiously descending on her, with the familiar by-products of powerlessness, paralysis, and self-loathing.

A few days later, Violetta, who is my friend and frequently comes up to Santa Barbara to attend my meditation retreats, gave me a call. "Can you help me?" she asked. "This old feeling of being stuck in molasses has taken me over again. The state of the world's climate makes me feel hopeless and irrelevant. I have stomach troubles again, with my belly feeling tight and nauseous. I'm worried about my health." Violetta told me that these symptoms had returned after she had seen the devastating article by the NASA scientist. "Maybe you can give me some practices that will help me get out of this hopeless cul-de-sac. Otherwise I'm useless and can't work."

My goal in working with Violetta was to teach her practices that would help her free herself from feelings of depression and self-deprecation so she could join with others in becoming active on behalf of the world. The first step was to help her make friends with herself again. Her current feeling of impotence had left her believing she was unworthy of regard—

her own or anyone else's. She needed to begin with the kindness of self-compassion.

Based on the Self-Compassion Practice, we devised phrases that would be helpful for Violetta during the days and weeks to come:

- May I hold myself with gentle care.
- May I hold myself with compassion, even when I feel defeated.
- May I extend tenderness toward myself, especially as I experience myself as vulnerable and inadequate.
- May I be able to reclaim respect for and friendship with myself.
- May I be free from suffering and all its causes.
- May I receive the support I need to continue my life with meaning and purpose.

Violetta felt that these phrases captured her experience. Feeling understood and supported, her inner sense of emptiness and deflation gave way to an increasing sense of inner determination.

Two days later, she paid me a visit. "I feel stronger now," she reported, "but still very overwhelmed by scary information and by my own knowledge of what the future could bring." Together we developed a brief meditation practice, especially useful at times when she had to sift through great amounts of difficult news on climate change. I had printed out one of the on-the-go practices on a card for Violetta:

⟿ WHEN I FEEL OVERWHELMED BY THE SUFFERING OF OTHERS OR OUR WORLD (WHICH IS A VERSION OF THE PRACTICE WHEN I FEEL OVERWHELMED BY ANOTHER'S PAIN)

1. In the face of overwhelming suffering, I bring my attention inward and downward into my body.
2. I notice my physical experience as felt in my body right now.
3. I bring my attention to my breath and exhale gently to relax.

4. I recognize my emotions and the felt sense of upset in my body.
5. With the out-breath, I allow myself to drop down into the physical sense of my experience and linger there for a little while.
6. I offer compassion to myself while continuing to breathe gently, holding this experience in my heart.
7. I once again direct my attention outward and turn toward the world, noticing what I am feeling and what I am seeing, ready to reconnect.

When I met Violetta again a few days later, she told me about her experience doing the practice she had followed on her card. "As I brought my attention inward and down into my body, I noticed that my jaw was tightly clenched and that I was feeling nauseous. Then I brought my attention to the movement of my breath and, in particular, to the sensations of the gentle release of the out-breath. I noticed that attending to exhaling in this way allowed me to relax, loosen, and let go a little. As I attended to what I was feeling about this recent piece of difficult news, I became aware of a mix of many different emotions. There were feelings of frustration and helplessness about having all these body symptoms and about feeling so inept. I also felt anxious about the possibility of sliding into a clinical depression. At the same time, there were feelings of deep sorrow for our world, and specifically worry about our drought here in California."

She continued, "As I contacted the felt sense, I consciously gave myself permission to be with what I was experiencing. There were sensations of vulnerability in my heart and great tightness in my stomach. Though it was uncomfortable to do so, I deliberately chose to let my awareness drop into these sensations, allowing myself to experience what I was feeling."

Checking the card, she went on, "After a few moments, I remembered that the next step was to offer compassion to myself. I immediately knew that I could not do this easily. I was feeling like a failure, and I could not access a sense of warmth or kindness toward myself. Instinctively, I put one hand on my heart and became aware of the gentle sensations of pressure on the wall of my chest. I put the other hand on my stomach and felt a great sense of vulnerability underneath all that tightness. As I did this, images came into my mind's eye of myself as a climate scientist. I saw myself arriving at my workplace prepared to do what I could to do, such as meaningful research and educate students, day after day, year after year. Then I continued to breathe gently while holding this experience lightly in my heart and belly. I observed how my body was breathing spontaneously, effortlessly, without my volition or control. For a few moments, I followed the gentle flow of the breath in this way. Slowly I began to feel kindness toward the person I am."

In the days that followed, Violetta felt a bit more confident, her mind became clearer, and creativity started to return. As she was no longer stuck with her own pain, she was now able to sit down and research the article she wanted to write. She slowly accepted that while she could commit herself wholeheartedly to doing work for the world, she may or may not be able to make a significant impact on behalf of the world climate or even the drought in California. Having begun to live with the truth of her own felt sense, she was now able to experience her feelings of defeat and being overwhelmed without falling into depression.

"It seemed that allowing myself to experience my feelings of frustration and sorrow for our world had unlocked something within me," she explained. "A knot in my heart and belly had loosened. I felt my chest expanding and my jaw softening. The deep helplessness and hopelessness I had felt gave way to something that was subtle and hard to name. While there was something timeless about this experience, as I brought my attention back to the here and now and the information about the world before me, I realized that it had only taken a minute or so. And yet even in that short time, something essential had come back into balance. A wave of warmth and concern for all life had swept through me."

In the next month, Violetta did write the article. She also managed to present her research at an important climate conference in Oslo. However, she knew that she would have to continue to work with her sense of discouragement and hopelessness. These were very old and persistent feelings for her. To support herself through times of desperation, she added the following Dissolving Hopelessness through Bodhichitta prayer to her morning practice:

⟜ DISSOLVING HOPELESSNESS THROUGH BODHICHITTA

- I notice the feelings of discouragement and despair in my body, and I recognize the discomfort I am experiencing.
- I choose to pause and feel the gentle breath of my heart.
- I offer compassion to myself and stay with the felt sense of my own suffering.
- I notice the stream of hopelessness and discouragement passing by, like thick, yellow sludge slowly curving down a tropical river.
- I let this slimy stream drift by with patience and acceptance.
- I remember that we all at times feel despair, fear, and grief, and also that all of us want to be happy.
- I include all those who have experienced despair and hopelessness in their work for this world in my prayer.
- I hold images of our suffering world in my mind's eye—polluted waters and skies, parched earth, distressed animals, and vulnerable humans.
- For our whole shared world, for the well-being and freedom of our world, I choose to wake up, to take care of my own despair.
- Then I can rest in the heart that cares for all.
- I can work on behalf of the two-legged, the four-legged, the winged, and the finned.
- I can wholeheartedly join others in their compassionate engagement.
- Grounding myself in the sensation of breath, I join the clear and immeasurable life-giving flow that interconnects us all.

Allowing herself to feel her despair helped Violetta slowly wash some of the sadness and grief out of her heart. Experiencing herself as part of a shared world and an interdependent part of life helped her to feel less burdened by her work. As she did her research and taught on behalf of the heart that cares for all, she was increasingly able to flow with both the times of grief and hopelessness and those of creativity and joy.

RELATED PRACTICES

The Self-Compassion Practice—Chapter 10, page 68
When I Feel Overwhelmed by Another's Pain practice—Chapter 15,
    page 37
The Heart that Cares for All (Bodhichitta) Practice—Chapter 12, pages
    88–89

JOURNAL EXERCISE

Sit down with a pencil and paper in a quiet place. Make yourself comfortable, rest in your gentle breath, and see what images and stories arise as you read the following prompts. If your own experiences come to mind, do some free writing.

1. Remember a time in your life when you felt overwhelmed by another person's pain or the world's pain. Describe the atmosphere, time of day, who was there, and what the feeling tone was. Do some free writing about it.

2. Imagine going through the steps of the practice When I Feel Overwhelmed by Another's Pain. Create an imaginary scenario of how the situation could have developed in an alternative way through this practice.

3. As you read over the The Heart That Cares for All (Bodhichitta) Practice, remember the time when you were overwhelmed by someone else's pain. Describe what comes up for you.

24

When Blending Families
Opens Wounds

This story describes the effort of bringing a big blended family together at a festive occasion. Such a get-together can bring up surprising emotional reactions and challenge your inner sense of balance. If you find yourself in the middle of such a situation, old wounds may burst open. The Heart's Intention, Self-Compassion, and Compassion for Others practices helped this couple survive a trying wedding.

Rita and Robert had flown to Hawaii to attend Robert's daughter Mary's wedding. Robert's ex-wife, Edith, with her big extended family and circle of friends, would also be at the wedding. Robert had left Edith in South Carolina ten years earlier to join Rita in Santa Barbara. The ripples caused by his leaving had gone far and deep and continued to reverberate in family dynamics.

Rita and Robert had been working with me in couple's counseling for the past two years. I had taught them Mindfulness Meditation and many practices that supported their marriage. However, the momentous nature of this wedding had ripped a tear in the delicate surface skin that had slowly grown over an old wound.

Outwardly everything seemed perfectly civilized when everyone met for the wedding. Previous spouses, family, and friends gathered and greeted each other. Everyone tried to be gracious and harmonious. Nonetheless, the pain still smoldering underneath was palpable. Rita and Robert tried to act calm and friendly, but inside they were churning. Rita became furiously sick with bronchitis, and Robert's back went out. Despite yoga and meditation in the morning, old sentiments kept creeping in, and they both felt demoralized to be subjected to old emotions such guilt, shame, resentment, and fear.

A few days into the wedding week, I received a phone call from Robert. "Can you meet Rita and me over Skype to help us regain some balance in the midst of all these difficult feelings that are coming up?" Robert paused and sighed. "Every time I see my ex-wife and ex-mother-in-law, I get this horrible feeling in my stomach."

The next morning when we met over Skype, Rita began, "I'm worried that Edith still hates me and is still hurting from Robert's abandonment. I'm afraid that those feelings will spill over and destroy this celebration." Robert confided that he felt grief about the years lost with his daughters as well as guilt about leaving them. Rita expressed how hard it was to be snubbed by some of Robert's old friends and how much shame she still felt about being the "other woman."

"Maybe it would be good," I said, "to clarify your heart's intentions. It seems to me that you feel confused and overwhelmed by all your conflicting feelings. With the Heart's Intention Practice, you can discern what is really important to you." I adapted the practice to address their particular challenges:

‍⌒ HEART'S INTENTION PRACTICE

When You Feel Confused

1. Sense your body.
2. Recognize with kindness the passing of thoughts and feelings of fear, self-doubt, and confusion.
3. Calm your heart with the gentleness of your out-breath.

4. Feel your own suffering and offer compassion to yourself.
5. Allow breath to move through your body ever so gently, connecting you to the bigger flow of life.
6. Recognize your deepest yearning for yourself, your extended family, and your new life together.
7. Sense your longing that your life may become aligned with a deeper meaning and purpose, with your heart's intention.
8. Feel the breath of your heart.
9. Know what would assist you to feel in balance again.
10. Allow breath to move through your body, for life to breathe you.

On the Skype call, I guided both Rita and Robert through this practice. When I inquired about what came up for Robert, he said, "As we did the practice, I realized that I want to find a way to stay present and connected with myself and Rita no matter how others relate to us."

Rita responded, "I want to be less afraid and more confident when I meet Robert's daughters and ex-wife. Then I can talk to them more naturally and allow for new ways to connect." She added quietly, "It was really difficult for me to feel self-compassion, as I still blame myself for the pain I caused after Robert moved to Santa Barbara to be with me. My heart's intention is to forgive myself one day so that I can live in peace again." They both expressed their hopes for a new kind of reconciliation between their new and old families.

A few days later, Rita, Robert, and I met on another Skype call. After listening to them both and hearing how family affairs continued to be superficially friendly yet tense underneath, I suggested the Self-Compassion Practice. I assured them that this practice was not about condoning or whitewashing possible mistakes that may have been made in the past; rather, it was meant to help them build a safe container for all their difficult feelings that were coming up.

"When we view ourselves with kindness and compassion," I explained, "we can look at and learn from whatever comes up for us."

Then I guided them through a Self-Compassion Practice. During this meditation, I suggested relevant phrases of compassion and forgiveness that Rita and Robert could offer to themselves:

- May I hold myself gently, compassionately, and with understanding.
- May I extend warmth to myself, especially when I feel self-blame.
- May I offer myself compassion as I try to step forward to make new relationships with the people I have been estranged from.
- May I hold the person I am now with kindness, while understanding how difficult it is to tolerate feelings of shame and guilt.
- May we all find peace of mind and heart as well as healing.

Rita reported how this practice allowed her to feel calmer and more peaceful, as the phrases released the most tightly held bonds of self-loathing. Robert told us that the phrases finally helped him to let go of some old resentment and imagine meeting his family with a little more flexibility and lightness. Once again we agreed to meet on Skype the next day.

At the next meeting, Rita reported that the night before she had sat at a table with one of the guests who described how complicated the wedding had been for him as he came in contact with members of his former wife's family who were also guests. As he told his story, old pain marked his face. Then someone else at the table chimed in, telling a very similar story of awkwardness and ache at a blended-family event.

After hearing about these shared difficulties, I suggested a Compassion for Others Practice to be offered to all those who suffer from blended-family complications:

- May all those at this wedding who are experiencing divided families be held with understanding and care.
- May all those in our country who suffer the fallout of separations, find peace again.
- May all people in this world who suffer shame, guilt, and anger

due to a family breakup find new, more peaceful ways of being with each other.
- May family celebrations, such as weddings, bar mitzvahs, or memorials be places of healing.

After doing this practice, Rita commented on how many blended families there are in this day and age. Spontaneously a feeling of warmth and care surged up in her for all those who are involved in divided situations. Rita and Robert both told me that this meditation had hit the "sweet spot" with its relevant and accessible phrases. Both of them were able to relax and let go a bit. When I began to expand the meditations beyond their own concerns and include the worries of others, they experienced their hearts becoming wider and healthier again. We decided to meet in person back home in Santa Barbara in four days' time.

When we met in my office, I asked Rita and Robert whether the way the wedding week finally unfolded was in any way aligned with their original heart's intentions. In response, Rita related the following story: "On the last evening, I saw five of Edith's women friends sitting at a table outside, chatting with each other during a luau. I gathered my courage and sat down at their table. I joined the conversation, and after a short time of initial awkwardness, more ease began to settle in. After a while, I was shocked when Edith joined the table as well, engaging in the conversation in a friendly way. My original heart's intention had been for a new way of relating in our extended family, and this was a small step in that direction."

RELATED PRACTICES

The Heart's Intention Practice—Chapter 9, page 57
The Self-Compassion Practice—Chapter 10, page 68
The Compassion for Others Practice—Chapter 11, pages 78–79

JOURNAL EXERCISE

Sit down with a pencil and paper in a quiet place. Make yourself comfortable, rest in your gentle breath, and see what images and stories arise as you read the following prompts. If your own experiences come to mind, do some free writing.

1. Remember a challenging family situation. Do some free writing about it.
2. Which of the mindfulness and compassion practices do you think would have helped you in this situation? Describe yourself doing this meditation.
3. Write a short story about how the problematic situation might have evolved following your use of some of the compassion practices.

25

Small Stories, Brief Practices, and Little Healings on the Go

WHEN I HAVE LOST MY BALANCE

Nora felt pushed away by her teenage daughter, and her inner upset led to desperate attempts to engage with her daughter. The practice for When I Have Lost My Balance helped her to ground herself in mindfulness and compassion, to relax a bit, and to accept *what is* without making things worse for herself and her daughter.

With nervous strides, Nora paced back and forth in her living room, checking her phone for text messages from her fifteen-year-old daughter, Kailye. She had not heard from Kailye in ten days, even though Nora had sent her daughter numerous messages and left little presents on the doorstep of the old family home, where her soon-to-be ex-husband and Kailye were still living.

Kailye had always been closer to her father, Tom. It seemed that the two shared the same jokes, sometimes at Nora's expense. As much as Nora had tried to improve her relationship with her daughter, successes were short-lived. Sometimes when Tom was out of town, mother and daughter got together and had a lovely time. Yet, in this triangle, Nora felt like she did not stand a chance, especially during the emotionally dangerous process of divorce.

After leaving gifts on her daughter's doorstep, Nora went shopping. To her surprise, she spotted Kailye with a friend at a department store. When Nora walked over to say hello, Kailye's smile vanished. She stiffened up and mumbled to her friend, "Let's get out of here!" Before Nora could engage with the girls, they had vanished into an elevator. For what seemed like an eternity, Nora stood by the elevator; tears began to run down her cheeks.

"Is something wrong?" a salesgirl asked.

"No, no," Nora answered, pulling herself together and trying to control her tears. Holding her handbag tightly clenched, she left as fast as she could.

Nora was tempted to run up the stairs to catch the girls and force a confrontation with Kailye. But she knew that everything she had done in desperation, from writing e-mails to forcing a meeting, had only made things worse. She knew that she had done everything she could for the moment and needed to find some inner place of acceptance and tranquility until a new chance to reconnect occurred naturally. Nora sat down on one of the benches in the shoe department and pulled a card out of her purse. At our last therapy meeting, I had given her the phrases from the When I Have Lost My Balance practice printed on that card.

Nora sat on the bench for a while. As she felt better and more at ease, she decided to go home and invite a friend over for dinner.

WHEN I DREAD CONTACT WITH ANOTHER

After his wife's death, Paul was left as a single father with his challenging teenage son. Grieving and stressed, he had come to dread the increasingly difficult encounters he had with his son. The Mindfulness On-the-Go practice When I Dread Contact with Another helped him to find his center again.

Paul's face and eyes looked tired, and he buried his hands in his ruffled black hair as he sat across from me during his weekly therapy visit. Paul's wife had recently died. Laura had been in her late thirties and passed away after a long battle with leukemia. Paul was now left with their thirteen-year-old son. Balancing a strenuous job in the financial world with child care, there was not much time left for himself. "I see myself getting short with Connor and would love to take some time out and go on retreat. But I have neither the time nor the money to get away," Paul told me.

Occasionally, when his mother came to town, Paul was able to come to our group's early evening meditation. But most helpful to him were the brief practices that he was able to work into his days. The practices I had recommended were relevant, accessible, and best of all, nonjudgmental. Paul often used the Mindful Pause cards I had given him earlier, especially when he started to feel upset or thrown off balance.

One day around lunchtime, Paul received a call from Connor's school principal, ordering Paul to come to his office. Connor had sprayed graffiti on several school walls. Paul was apprehensive about meeting with the unduly harsh principal. But even more, he dreaded a confrontation with Connor.

Paul went outside and sat on one of the benches behind his office building. After taking his tie and jacket off, he got out his phone and pulled up the Mindful Pause website. Scrolling down, he found the Mindfulness On-the-Go practice he needed.

⊸ WHEN I DREAD CONTACT WITH ANOTHER

1. I notice the sensations in my body.
2. I exhale gently to relax.
3. I recognize my aversion to engaging with the other.
4. I sense the breath of my heart.
5. I pause to offer compassion to myself and hold my own unease with kindness.

6. I notice that the other and I ultimately want to be happy and allow for the possibility of meeting the other with peace and respect.
7. I sense the touch between my feet and the ground, and feel my connection with the earth and the world around me.

Paul felt how tight his shoulders and jaw were. Just noticing the strength and authenticity of those feelings allowed him to feel more grounded. He made a conscious intention to interrupt the process of his mind racing and his anger welling up. Tuning in to the movements and sensations of his natural out-breath slowly allowed Paul to feel more calm. He experienced each out-breath as dropping a little deeper than before.

He began to offer some thoughts of compassion for himself:

- May I hold myself with care, even when things are difficult.
- May I be gentle with myself as I go through this upsetting afternoon.

The tension began to subside and gave way to sadness. In his mind's eye, he saw his wife's face showing a warm glow. For a while, he stayed with the feeling of sorrow in his heart. Then he became aware of the nearby maple trees, which were starting to change color in the fall weather.

Something shifted, and Paul realized how upset and angry Connor must be about having lost his mom as well as the family he had known. Underneath it all, Paul knew that Connor wanted to be happy again.

Paul took a few more minutes before going to the office; he decided to walk between the trees, back and forth, for three minutes. Very slowly he put one foot in front of the other, intently sensing the contact between the soles of his feet and the ground.

This exercise helped him to be in the present moment, away from worries and fears, in the here and now. In the spirit of the on-the-go practice, he stood still for a moment, felt his feet on the ground and the ground supporting him. He breathed in the crisp autumn air. There was even a sense of comfort coming from the trees, with their branches moving in the breeze ever so slightly. Paul felt a little more ready to face what he dreaded and to accept the challenges of the afternoon ahead.

That evening, Paul and Connor finally had a long talk. After getting a burger together, they went for a hike up a local mountain trail. At first they did not speak, and Connor seemed sullen. For about a half an hour, they silently climbed the trail, Connor leaving Paul behind. Paul's heart sank, and he felt discouraged. *He is leaving me*, Paul thought.

Yet up on the hilltop, Paul was surprised to see Connor leaning against a tree, with just the smallest smile on his face. On the way down, they began to talk about Laura. They shared some stories and memories and confessed how much they both missed her.

Paul told me the following week that the on-the-go practice had surely helped him make this contact with Connor and helped make a new healing phase in their relationship possible.

Just the night before our session, Connor had said to Paul, "Let's walk that trail more often." Then he'd added, "And we should get a big dog to walk with us."

"Great idea," Paul had agreed.

WHEN I AM CONFUSED

Maria was a nurse who felt wrenched between choices: enjoying a fun social activity or helping a suffering patient. Often your personal and professional lives meet such crossroads, which can be troubling. The Heart's Intention Practice helps you clarify your deeper intentions and the goals that support them.

Michael and I had been presenting at a palliative care conference on the role of mindfulness and compassion practices in end-of-life care. Maria and I had met at this forum the previous year. When we talked during this year's conference, Maria told me about her current work in hospice and how hard yet rewarding she found the work. She also told me about her mindfulness practice and the meditation group she was attending regularly.

Then she proceeded to tell me the following story: "One Friday afternoon I was sitting at the nurse's station, which borders the hospice ward," she said. "I was tired after a long day on the ward and was drinking my third cup of coffee of the afternoon. A friend and colleague had texted me, 'Come to room 334 at 5:00 P.M. to celebrate Susan's birthday.'" Maria smiled at me and said, "I wanted nothing more than a good piece of chocolate cake. I knew that would give me the energy I needed to finish the day at work and to make dinner for my three rascals at home."

She looked thoughtful as she continued, "Then I remembered Patrick, the patient with the inoperable colon cancer in room 326." Maria sighed. "Patrick was a fifty-five-year-old man who just a few months before had received an unexpected diagnosis of colon cancer. The doctor had given him a prognosis of two months to live. But Patrick was not at all ready to die. The pain in his body as well as his worry for himself and his teenage daughter kept him in a state of agitation and distress. One of the only moments that gave him some relief at this point was when I came to his room to do healing touch and a little bit of mindful breathing with him."

Maria continued, "I knew that Patrick wanted me to visit him to put my hands on his aching stomach. For a moment I didn't know what to do: chocolate cake or sitting at Patrick's bedside. It was 4:45, and the birthday party was at 5:00. I would be off work at 5:30. I felt torn. Then I remembered one of your talks from last year, when you had told us about intention. You had talked about the difficulty in finding our heart's intention and offered us a way to get there."

Our minds can often be confused and may not always give us the right answers. It is important that we trust our deeper intuitive knowing, the knowing that comes from our hearts. Then our practical goals will be aligned with a deeper meaning in our lives.

Maria began to rummage in her purse. Then she smiled at me coyly and pulled out the little piece of paper on which she had scribbled the steps of an on-the-go Heart's Intention Practice.

The paper said:

⊸ AN ON-THE-GO VERSION OF THE
HEART'S INTENTION PRACTICE

When You Feel Confused

1. I sense my body.
2. I exhale gently to relax.
3. I hold an image of myself, confused and at a loss.
4. I feel my heart and offer compassion to myself.
5. I sense my heart's intention.
6. I recognize that my heart's intentions can inform the setting of tangible goals.
7. I rest in my breath and accept what arises.

Maria continued her story. "On the evening of the birthday party, I was the only one at the nursing station, and things were momentarily quiet. I took a few minutes to myself and did that little meditation. As I sensed my body, I realized how tired and heavy I felt. At the same time, the out-breath brushing through my chest felt soothing to me. After about three out-breaths, I began to feel lighter; the load was starting to lift from my soul. I saw images in my mind's eye: myself sitting at the nursing desk, the kids at home, the chocolate cake. There was also Patrick, the fine lines in his face revealing his distress. I felt him waiting for me to come to his room."

Maria went on. "Then I felt my own heart, at first a little tight, then increasingly tender and a bit raw. I began to offer compassion toward myself and said silently,

• May I be able to hold my life chores with patience and gentle care.
• May I find the support I need so I can be there for others."

Maria sat quietly for a while. Then she added, "I was thinking of myself and Patrick, and I whispered,

• May both of us find the sustenance we need to live our heart's intention, even when things are difficult.
• May life rise up to meet us both."

Maria drew her story to an end. "My heart felt drawn to Patrick, and I knew that I would feel more at peace with myself after I had sat with him, even if it was just for fifteen minutes. I was surprised that I felt very clear now, and even the chocolate cake had lost its appeal. I knew that the sugar high would not ultimately make me feel better.

"Practicing When I Am Confused had been so useful to me. For a while I sat in my chair, experiencing my feelings. Surrendering to the breath for a little while gave me a sense of refuge, of now, a place that was totally my own in the midst of the interconnected web of life. Now it wasn't difficult to accept my inner answer."

RELATED PRACTICES

When I Have Lost My Balance—Chapter 15, page 137
When I Dread Contact with Another—Chapter 15, pages 136–37
When I Feel Confused—Chapter 9, page 57

JOURNAL EXERCISE

Sit down with a pencil and paper in a quiet place. Make yourself comfortable, rest in your gentle breath, and see what images and stories arise as you read the following prompts. If your own experiences come to mind, do some free writing.

1. Think of a time when you felt rejected by someone close to you. Do some free writing. Imagine using one of the Mindfulness On-the-Go practices. What feelings came up?
2. Think of a time when you feared interacting with someone. If it feels right, use the practice When I Dread Contact with Another and reflect on that experience.
3. Think of a time when you were torn between two choices and felt utterly confused. Describe what might have happened if you had used the When I Feel Confused practice.

CONCLUSION
Walking on the Mountain

In the scorching heat of August 1983, I found myself traveling in the mountains near the town of Rishikesh in northern India. Rishikesh is a midsized town adjoining the river Ganges, which flows down the Himalayan foothills as a majestic bluish-brown stream. I was twenty-five and on my second trip to India.

On this particular day, I was hiking up a mountain to the village of Neelkanth, searching for an ancient and sacred shrine dedicated to Lord Shiva. Shiva embodies the dynamic of change, of destruction and renewal. In my always drastically changing life, I felt drawn to experience this energy. Without a map, hiking gear, or even water, I set out on my path; my only accessories were curiosity and a longing for meaning.

I had not expected the August sun to become blazing hot so rapidly. It was as if the vibrating, glimmering heat was standing still like an invisible wall right in front of my eyes. At first I felt a vague anxiety; this soon increased to bewilderment and fear. As I felt more and more uncertain about the trail, I was swept with a cold panic.

Around 11:00 A.M., a quarter of the way up to Neelkanth, I collapsed under a red tree shrub barely able to cover me with shade. It was too hot to go on and too hot to go back. As I grew increasingly dazed, I decided that my only choice was to wait until late afternoon, hoping that by then the temperature would become slightly cooler.

In a stupor, I crouched under my flimsy bush. I felt my heart pounding. Then everything became very still. After I had been there for maybe an hour, I began to notice the space around me, the sandy ground, the beautiful patterns in the bark of the shrub, the light catching in the tiny leaves, and the few red berries peeking out from between the sparse foliage. Finally, I found the feeling of my breath and began to notice the sensation and motion of the soothing in-breath and a sense of relief with the out-breath. Strangely, I was not panicked any more. Then I felt something like a kick on my back.

I looked around in surprise. A small, thin Indian man with no legs and only one arm stood on the path staring at me. He was leaning forward on a pair of wooden crutches which he used as he hobbled along on leg stumps. More surprising still, he appeared quite agile and strong. He looked at me with fierce black eyes. "You stay, you die. You get up!" he announced firmly, prodding me with his crutch.

Very reluctantly, I got to my feet. The situation was embarrassing. I was much taller and considerably better nourished than this man, yet he was the one with all the energy. With his one arm, he took my sleeping roll and flung it over his shoulder. With his stick, he pointed, saying, "You go," allowing for no objections. This nameless, legless, nearly armless man shepherded me sternly up the mountain.

Through the little man's broken pigeon English, I found out that he had traveled from Delhi in the hope of completing a pilgrimage to the ancient Shiva temple. He owned a roadside cigarette stall with his three brothers and had lost his limbs many years earlier in an electrical accident. Despite his physical trials, he seemed in great spirits. "Chew," he ordered, handing me roots he dug up along the way for moisture.

Many hours later, after he had successfully herded me up the mountain, we reached our goal, Neelkanth. Wanting nothing from me (in fact, he barely allowed me to buy him his day's meal), we shared rice and dal, a simple Indian dish, in a tea stall near the village.

The spontaneous compassion of the pilgrim possibly saved my life. Moreover, this amazing man left me with an example that I find myself returning to over and over as I live my life. I regard him as an important teacher for me—and maybe for you, as you work with the practices presented in this book. With his fierce compassion, my mountain guide taught me determination, courage, faith, and a lot of patience.

Looking back over these many decades since I was first mesmerized by the eyes of the ancient monk in Sri Lanka, I see a pattern. The trials and inspiration I encountered climbing up the stony mountain to Neelkanth have been echoed in the challenges and perseverance I have experienced during my years of learning.

Mindfulness has given me the scaffolding, the stability to sit with strong feelings and find peace and compassion within myself, the nourishing attitude necessary to embark on my unlikely journey. Caring and gentleness, coupled with discipline, helped me do the inner work of healing and transformation. Self-compassion made it possible to look inward and tolerate what I found, and ultimately to make friends with myself. An attitude of warmth toward myself assisted me in seeing that my life was on safe ground; I was able to gather the fragments and calm the frightened child within. With the safety born of self-compassion, I was able to see my anger, depression, and, most of all, fear, yet now I viewed them with tender, understanding eyes. As I have continued my practice in mindfulness and compassion, including considerable psychological work, I have drawn on the example of the pilgrim in Rishikesh, especially at times when I have been tempted to give up.

Thirty-five years after I began to walk up the mountain to the shrine of Shiva, I am now walking down the mountain, trying to bring my practice into daily life, tilling what I have learned into the ground of daily experience. This summer I walked the Camino, an ancient Christian pilgrimage path in Spain. Beginning in the Pyrenees in France and continuing to Santiago de Compostela in northern Spain, this path has been walked by pilgrims seeking to encounter the sacred for fifteen hundred years. More than two hundred thousand pilgrims walk the

Camino annually. Some of them are Catholic, some are Jews or Prot-
estants, and some are agnostic or follow other persuasions. People join
the Camino, the Way, from all walks of life. Many are at crossroads,
with pain in their hearts or at a loss about what to do and seeking to
find inner direction.

I walked the Camino with my daughter, Bella; my husband, Michael;
and his brother Phil, a Catholic priest, who was our guide on the trip.
One of my German cousins and some friends also joined us. We trekked
about fifteen to twenty miles a day, wandering on beautiful paths through
villages, forests, and meadows, past ripe fields and fruit orchards, and
along rivers. We stayed in hostels in the evenings. There was a beautiful
dawn sky when we set out in the early morning and scorching heat in the
middle of the day. There were some rainy days when we walked with wet
shoes, protected only by plastic capes, and there were days with beautifully cloudy skies, giving us shelter from the August sun.

There were ten days of walking with blisters and exhaustion and, for
me, the discomfort caused by an inherent problem with my ankle. Along
the way, I was confronted with my past. Walking with my cousin brought
up many feelings about my birth family that I had to grapple with.
Walking with Phil stirred up the wounds I had received in my relationship with the Catholic Church. I began to feel frustrated with Phil and
some of his readings. I was reminded of the impact the church had had
on my life, costing me two years in an orphanage due to my mother's fear
of her Catholic family. The pervasive shame and alienation I carried had
ultimately prompted me to leave my mother and her medical clinic, as
well as my family and country, to follow my path to healing. My mind
became consumed with these thoughts.

During each early morning meditation on the Camino, I offered kind
attention to my own worries and fears, as well as compassion toward the
struggling person I have been these many years. I realized that I needed
to forgive myself again and again, each time a little bit more, and that
forgiveness is not all or nothing but needs to be approached slowly and
carefully. Working with the practices of self-compassion and self-forgiveness

as well as compassion and forgiveness for others felt like letting go of a heavy burden.

As I walked the Camino and struggled with old memories and shame, I came to a full stop. I realized that I had to find my inner resources. I returned once again to the practices I have been developing over the years. I included in my prayers all those in this world who are criticized or persecuted on moral grounds and are alone in their anguish, as well as those who, because of their loyalty, are caught in rigidity and judgment. Then I began to feel the kind of peace that comes from applying the right medicine. I had been waiting for healing from the outside, such as for the church to abandon its harsh dogmas. Healing for me needed to begin inside.

My struggles on this Camino with my root tradition, which is Catholicism, led me to understand that I ultimately cannot get rid of my deep, deep wounds, but I can slowly modify my response to them.

You might ask yourself, "How long will my wounds be running the show?" The essential steps of the practices presented in this book are noticing, sensing, feeling, self-compassion, coming back to breath, and integrating back to life. As triggers carry you away into your old traumas, you can always come back to being present by feeling your feet on the ground and the breath in your nostrils. When you are challenged and old patterns flair up, you will be able to see them as stepping-stones to inner happiness and freedom.

The Camino, the inner and outer one, is about opening with kindness to everything you meet, including your old shame, confusion, and hurt. This process moves like a spiral, with a widening arc of compassion, where more and more is included, and less and less is excluded from your heart.

During the last few days, we walked down from on high to see the sprawling city, skyscrapers, and to the east, a huge gray factory. We realized that our journey was about coming down the other side of the mountain, about descending into ordinary, busy, everyday life again.

Among pilgrims on the Camino, there was an etiquette of kindness;

of spontaneous acts of friendliness; and an unspoken, maybe even unconscious, attitude of compassion. I was reminded of the fierce compassion with which the Indian pilgrim had shepherded me up the path in India. Now walking down the gentle slopes in Spain seemed more gradual. I realized that we are secretly yearning to extend our kindness beyond ourselves, our families, and our tribes. Deep inside we may be longing to transcend our habits of primarily protecting the near and dear or the members of the group with which we are identified. I propose that we have an internal wish to be kind to more people than those in our little group. Yet most of us do not know how to expand beyond that, because it is the social convention to be protective, competitive, standoffish, suspicious, and ambitious.

Science proposed the selfish gene. But there may be another inherent possibility within us, one that is waiting for us below the reptilian and tribal aspects of our nature. There may be the "Camino gene." Buddhists may call this buddha-nature and summon bodhichitta, or the heart that cares for all. Christians may summon their Christ nature and mystical Jews, their "I and thou-ness," while Native Americans commit to "all my relations." I suggest that something in us longs to join those wider, more spacious and heartfelt orbits of wise compassion. We all have a yearning to live our natural potential for compassion that we carry within us. It is just a matter of what has been asleep needing to be reawakened.

Phil, the priest, is looking for ways to give everyone, without exception, the chance to partake in the Camino. He is planning to take a group of people with mental and physical disabilities in wheelchairs to the Camino next year, so they also can follow the pilgrim's path. The Camino is only one of the many ways that we can wake up to find meaning, freedom, and love. Last year, when I joined the Kalachakra celebrations with the Dalai Lama in Ladakh, he stated, "My religion is compassion." The 110,000 Tibetans who had come from China, Bhutan, India, and Nepal were joined by 5,000 people like me from the West to hear his message of the heart that cares for all. A year later the pope, speaking to the US Congress about the need to end poverty and take care of the many refugees and immigrants in this world, as well as our mother earth, affirmed the same message of boundless caring.

And you and I will be living our distinctive ways of opening our hearts in our personal lives. My students and clients whom you met in this book have tapped into this benevolent field of compassion that is always there for us. I think of Christina, who as an educator of immigrant children touches the lives of so many families. I think of Gregory, who is now transforming ugly urban projects into affordable, sustainable living spaces. I appreciate Maria and Michael, who tirelessly share their kindness with those who are dying, and Larry, Nora, and Paul, who, having found some healing, can be more loving parents to their children. The power of small acts spreads outward, as when you throw a stone into a pond, and the ripples open their reach in widening circles.

ACKNOWLEDGMENTS

Recognizing that behind each single event are countless causes and conditions that made them happen, I know that I will miss many people as I say "thank you."

Foremost I want to thank His Holiness the Dalai Lama for his teachings, which inspired me during the past seven years to write this book. Then I want to thank my mentor, Jack Kornfield, who encouraged me to write *Heartwork*. Jack's faith in me and our many discussions helped me to find the courage to teach and write.

Further I want to express my gratitude to my guide and inspirational teacher, Joanna Macy, who inspired me to understand the importance of bodhichitta and our responsibility for the welfare of all sentient beings, especially our world.

I am deeply thankful to Barbara Gates, my developmental editor, whose guidance, teaching, diligence, and friendship have made this journey possible for me. Her bright and loving spirit carried me through.

I want to thank my husband, Michael, who has been my muse and sounding board, always eager to help me think through spiritual and philosophical challenges. I want to thank my son Joshua, who designed charts, gave encouragement, and patiently delivered countless manuscripts for me. I want to thank Lisa Robertson and my son Ben, who helped me design some of the original charts. I am grateful to Ben for bringing me to H.H. the Dalai Lama and for creating the first "MAMA chant." My daughter, Bella, contributed with ideas for some of the stories.

Further I want to thank the many clients and students of my meditation groups, who helped me learn how to teach and how to make Buddhist practices accessible and relevant.

I want to thank Juliet Spohn-Thomei and Anne Price from La Casa de Maria Retreat Center, who gave me the opportunity to teach the many retreats and seminars that would become the foundation for my practices. I want to thank La Casa de Maria Retreat Center and the Museum of Natural History in Santa Barbara, who trusted me to teach for many years now on their premises.

There were many generous people who read parts of the manuscript and gave me feedback, such as Elaine McCracken, Antonia Robertson, Jean Weininger, Joshua Weininger, Bella Weininger, Annette Zurhausen Vaz Pinto, Catherine Gauthier-Downes, Ellen Taylor, Philip Black, and others. I thank them deeply.

I want to thank my agent, Johanna Maghool from Waterside Publications, and my patient Shambhala editors, Kathleen Gregory and Breanna Locke. I also want to acknowledge and thank the many people who guided and challenged me during the past many years, as this provided the fertile ground to learn to love and to grow.

Lastly I want to thank Lucy, my sweet Chihuahua-mix lady; Malenka, the springer spaniel; and Kitty, the feisty cat, who all kept me company during the long late evenings of writing.

APPENDIX
Charts

Compassionate Choice Practice

TRIGGER
Something happens that sparks an immediate uncomfortable feeling. This trigger can be set off by internal thoughts and feelings or by external events.

SENSATION
Our body responds instantaneously. We may experience, for example, a tightening in our belly, a constriction near our heart, or a flushed face.

EMOTION
Feelings that come up may be anger, fear, sadness, embarrassment, indignation, or some other unpleasant emotion.

AUTOMATIC ASSOCIATION
Moods, memories, and images from our past arise and entangle us and intensify emotions.

EMOTIONAL CONCLUSION
Consciously or unconsciously, we form beliefs about ourselves, others, and our world which seem convincing.

URGE TO ACT
We experience a great deal of tension, which can be externalized as an intense desire to fix the situation or internalized as intense rumination.

Mindful Time-Out

We choose to interrupt the reactive process with an activity that restores our inner balance. We notice the sensations and emotions of more tenderness and quiet.

COMPASSIONATE AWARENESS
We notice our reaction to the trigger with compassion for ourselves and others.

SENSATIONS & EMOTIONS OF COMPASSION
We feel the sensations and emotions when expanding our care to ourselves and others.

COMPASSIONATE EVALUATION
We gain a wider perspective and can consider a range of possibilities.

COMPASSIONATE CHOICE
We respond with more awareness, skill, and care.

RESULTING SENSATIONS & EMOTIONS
We feel the sensations and emotions having made a compassionate choice. We may feel increased relaxation, physical wellness, aliveness, and an improved connection with others.

OUTCOME
New response patterns can develop and our relationship to ourselves and others improve.

Compassionate Choice Practice Worksheet

TRIGGER

SENSATION

EMOTION

AUTOMATIC ASSOCIATION

EMOTIONAL CONCLUSION

URGE TO ACT

Mindful Time-Out

COMPASSIONATE AWARENESS

SENSATIONS & EMOTIONS OF COMPASSION

COMPASSIONATE EVALUATION

COMPASSIONATE CHOICE

RESULTING SENSATIONS & EMOTIONS

OUTCOME

NOTES

PART ONE *My Story*

1. John Welwood, *Toward a Psychology of Awakening: Buddhism, Psychotherapy, and the Path of Personal and Spiritual Transformation* (Boston: Shambhala, 2000).
2. The Dalai Lama, *The Compassionate Life* (New York City: Books Squared, 2009).

PART TWO *Nine Practices for Cultivating Compassion*

1. Jack Kornfield, *The Art of Forgiveness, Lovingkindness and Peace* (New York City: Bantam Dell, 2003).
2. Eugene Gendlin, *Focusing* (New York City: Bantam, 1981).
3. Jon Kabat-Zinn, *Coming to Our Senses: Healing Ourselves and the World Through Mindfulness* (New York City: Hyperion, 2005).
4. Pema Chödrön, *How to Meditate* (Louisville, CO: Sounds True, 2013).
5. B. Alan Wallace, "Settling the Body in Its Natural State," from *48 Guided Meditations* (CD).

6. Robert Bly, trans., *The Kabir Book: Forty-Four of the Ecstatic Poems of Kabir* (Boston: Beacon Press, 2007).

7. Thich Nhat Hanh, *Present Moment Wonderful Moment: Mindfulness Verses for Daily Living*, 2nd ed. (Berkeley, CA: Parallax Press, 2002).

8. John Welwood, "Between Heaven and Earth: Principles of Inner Work," *Toward a Psychology of Awakening: Buddhism, Psychotherapy, and the Path of Personal and Spiritual Transformation* (Boston: Shambhala, 2000).

9. The Dalai Lama, *The Compassionate Life* (New York City: Books Squared, 2009).

10. Kristin Neff, *Self-Compassion: The Proven Power of Being Kind to Yourself* (New York City: William Morrow, 2011).

11. Mary Oliver, *Dream Work* (New York City: Atlantic Monthly Press, 1986).

12. Joanna Macy and Molly Young Brown, *Coming Back to Life: Practices to Reconnect Our Lives, Our World* (Gabriola Island, BC, Canada: New Society, 1998).

13. Ibid.

14. The Dalai Lama, *The Art of Happiness* (London: Penguin Publishing Group, 2009).

15. Daniel J. Siegel, *Mindsight: The New Science of Personal Transformation* (New York City: Bantam, 2010).

PART THREE *Stories*

1. Pema Chödrön, "The Propensity to Be Bothered: Working with the Causes of Suffering," podcast from Pema Osel Ngak Choling Retreat Center, Vermont, May 2011.

2. Sharon Salzberg, *Faith: Trusting Your Own Deepest Experience* (New York City: Riverhead, 2002).

INDEX

intention, xvii, xviii, 111, 114
  bodhichitta and, 34, 82–83
  clarifying, 88, 211–14
  to forgive, 118, 163
  on the go, 210
  and goals, relationship of, 53–54,
    57–58
  to offer compassion, 72, 75–76
  for self-care, 31
  See also aspiration
interbeing, 74, 86
interconnectedness, xvi, xvii, 77, 83,
    87–88, 127
interdependence, 7, 34, 70–71,
    77–78, 199
intuition, 16, 21, 111

Jewish mysticism, 222
journal exercises, xvii–xviii, 144
  on anger and rage, 185
  on bodhichitta, 91
  on compassion, 21, 27, 69, 81
  on confusion, 60, 215
  on family issues, 206
  on forgiveness, 27, 122, 165
  on internal divisions, 192
  on life and spiritual practice, 16
  on Mindfulness and Loving
    Awareness meditations, 45
  on mindfulness in daily life, 139
  on painful patterns, 158
  on rejection, 215
  on relationships, 165, 173
  on self-criticism, 151

on spiritual experiences and
    turning points, 8
  on suffering in early life, 12
  on transforming reactivity, 52
  on triggers, 109
  when overwhelmed by another's
    pain, 200

Kabat-Zinn, Jon, 36
Kabir, 37
Kalachakra celebration, 222
Karma Yoga, 6
Kashepa, Bante, 5
kindness, 221–22
  in Heart's Intention Practice, 57,
    58–59
  mindfulness and, 36, 38, 42
  in on-the-go practices, 125,
    136–37, 138
  self-compassion and, xiv, xvii, 64,
    66–67, 150, 195, 203–4
  toward oneself, 167, 180, 197
  toward others, 25, 35, 70, 73
  See also loving-kindness
Kornfield, Jack, 15, 19–20, 32

loneliness, 17, 57, 64, 127, 136
love, 5–6, 62, 138, 190
  for all beings, 83–84, 88–89, 119
  definition of, 62
  developing, 17–18
  difficulties as asset to, 23–24
  forgiveness and, 111–12
  foundation for, xix